To our friend
Hank Webster, who
would rather hunt
than work

Jack Dow
&
Jim Robinson

HUNTING ADVENTURES

— With Jimmy Robinson

Highlights of Hunting Experiences over a Span of Fifty Years
as Related by the Associate Editor of *Sports Afield* Magazine

Publishers

T. S. DENISON & COMPANY

Minneapolis, Minnesota

Dedicated to Bob Peters,
a great hunter and sportsman who gave me the
inspiration to write this book.

Introduction

During the many years that I have known the author of this book, there is one incident about him that stands out vividly in my memory. It reveals a great deal about the man — what he is and what he does.

It concerns a certain monthly expense report that he sent to me after one of his shooting expeditions. In running a magazine such as *Sports Afield*, I examine many expense accounts of our staff which is routine procedure. But the report I received from Jimmy was unusual. It simply read: "Trip to Cuba — $35."

Glancing at it, I was struck with the realization that Jimmy Robinson is the only man I know who is resourceful enough to spend two weeks in Cuba shooting doves, quail and ducks for less money than it costs to buy half a case of shells.

Jimmy's capabilities make him an ideal outdoorsman and hunter. He has unbridled energy. He is an encyclopedia of knowledge about almost every phase of the outdoors. And he has friends by the hundreds. I've never met a man who knew Jimmy that didn't like him. And I never expect to meet a man who will speak an unkind word about him.

His many resources have made him one of the key men on the *Sports Afield* staff for thirty-four years. His writing assignments have taken him all over the world hunting many kinds of game, from trophy-sized African lions to Georgia quail. When Jimmy talks about hunting even the expert hunters listen. They know that this man has had the experience in every type of hunting. In fact, if you listen to him reminisce about his past exploits, you will discover that he has pioneered in every phase of hunting and shooting.

All this experience certainly has qualified him to write this book. In it he has compressed fifty years of hunting which runs the full gamut of upland game, waterfowl and big game. It is replete with anecdotes, such as only Jimmy's wide travels and experiences could produce. It is a book for and about shooters, including Annie Oakley, Ad Topper-

4

wein, Ernest Hemingway and many other present-day scattergun celebrities. Jimmy has shot with the best of them.

More than that, this book is a compendium of how-to-do-it information on all phases of hunting, including the sporting arms that hunters carry and the art of hitting what you aim at. When you have read the chapters about African big game hunting, as well as hunting wild turkey, quail, ducks and geese, or Canadian moose, you will know as much as you need to know to make the book pay for itself in giving you greater skill. If you're a skeet shooter, a trapshooter, or a live pigeon gunner, here you will find authoritative and tested techniques to help you become an expert marksman.

Jimmy Robinson is eminently qualified to write this book because of his fifty years of hunting adventures. Shortly after he was discharged from the 44th Canadian Infantry Battalion in Winnipeg, following World War I, he played baseball and hockey in Manitoba, and later in North Dakota. He even taught school for a year in Manitoba.

Eventually he migrated to Chicago where he joined the Amateur Trapshooting Association in 1922. Here he reported his first Grand American Trapshoot in Chicago in 1923 with the late Walter Eckersall, all-American football great, formerly with the Chicago Tribune, and Leo Fischer of the Chicago American. Two years later Jimmy joined *Sports Afield* to become Associate Editor under Joe Godfrey, then publisher of the magazine.

No matter where Jimmy may travel around the country during the year, each fall finds him at his duck camp on the Delta marsh in Manitoba where he has hunted since boyhood. It has been my privilege to gun there with him.

I recall the excellent instruction I received from this expert on my first visit to his camp. I discovered that I had much to learn about duck shooting. The time was shortly before dawn. Jimmy and I were shooting out of a boat drawn into the rushes. Suddenly a flight of canvasbacks came in and I fired. To my amazement, three ducks fell. It was, of course, a freak lucky shot. But I saw Jimmy cock a sidelong glance that clearly said, "Oh, so we're going to have a little contest, eh?" From then on he gave me a lesson on shooting ducks that I will never forget.

Ever since that day I have observed several rules that I learned to follow whenever I have hunted with him. I consider it my duty to fellow hunters to pass them on whenever I can.

The first rule is never to get into a duck shooting contest with him. The second is never to argue with him about *who* shot *what* score at *what* skeet or trapshoot, or *when* — because you know you will lose. The third rule is that under no circumstances permit him to trap you into playing poker. You will be the loser. The fourth and most important rule is — to see as much as you can of this exceptional man.

Outdoorsmen are a pretty nice breed of guys, but even against such tough competition, Jimmy Robinson is outstanding. This book is a tribute to his successful career as a hunter, shooter and sportsman.

—Ted Kesting,
Editor, *Sports Afield* Magazine

ACKNOWLEDGEMENTS

I have appreciated the generous cooperation of my hunting friends who have contributed their photographs to illustrate the chapters in this book. Especial recognition is given to the well-known wildlife artists, Roger Preuss and Les Kouba, who have released their paintings to me for reproduction in this book.

Contents

CHAPTER ONE

SERENGETI
SAFARI

The rhythmic snoring of my tent mates had nearly lulled me to sleep when out of the black and chilly night came the most unearthly sound I had ever heard. It was the wail of a banshee, the scream of a tortured man, and the laugh of a lunatic, all rolled into one. I sat bolt upright, startled and apprehensive. The snoring stopped and George Hart shifted under his blankets. Then he raised himself on one elbow, listening. If Pat Hemingway was awake, he gave no indication.

"My God, what is that?" George spoke in an anxious whisper.

Pat revealed that he was awake. "Just a hyena. They must have found our bait."

The single anguished shriek now was followed by a whole chorus of fiendish sounds that rent the night with indescribable horror. To George and me, newcomers in Africa, it sounded like a dirge from another world.

Then this cacophony of sound was split by a tremendous roar. It seemed to me that I could feel its vibrations even within the tent. The back of my neck tingled with its chilling effect. Another roar, louder and closer, followed the first. The hyena devil chorus was stilled for a moment, then erupted again. But now it was farther away. The sounds finally ebbed into the night and the world was quiet again.

9

"Now you can go to sleep again," Pat said quietly. "A couple of lions have driven the hyenas from the bait."

This was my introduction to the African scene, and all I had read or heard about it had not prepared me for this moment. Words are simply inadequate to describe the unreality of the sounds hyenas make when driven by lions from bait on which they hope to feast.

The thrill of the chase has coursed through my veins for as long as I can remember. But somehow I had never thought of lion hunting in Africa. Now here I was, lying awake at night in a camp at the edge of the vast Serengeti Plain, listening to the gibberish of a hyena pack and the roar of a pair of lions. There was a quality of unreality in the situation. I thought back about how I had happened to be here.

The origin of this African safari dated back one year to a duck hunt in Cuba. Bob Naegele and I were visiting my friend Ernest Hemingway at his Cuban estate. We had returned to his house after a wonderful morning shooting teal with Armando Pessino which we had hunted from tree blinds at the edge of a marsh.

"You ought to go to Africa," Papa Hemingway said as we settled down to some cool rum punches mixed by Papa's wife, Mary. "Shoot yourself a lion before you get too fat and too old and too feeble."

He had a son who could make arrangements. Pat had left medical school and a promising career as a physician to settle in Africa. Now he was a white hunter for an Englishman named Russell Bowker-Douglass, who owns Tanganyika Tours and Safaris, Ltd., of Arusha.

Back in Minneapolis the idea of making a trip to Africa increasingly occupied my mind. Finally I suggested it to Jack Dow one day when he was hunting with me at our Delta Marsh duck camp in Manitoba.

"I'll go," he said, "and I'll get your pal Ray Hickok in Rochester, N. Y., to go with us. Who'll we get for the fourth?"

"Me," said George Hart. Busy cleaning his gun, he had eavesdropped our conversation.

Later, at the National Skeet shoot in Reno, movie director Toby Anguish put in a clincher. "You won't go wrong with Bowker-Douglass. He's one of the top safari men in Africa. Gave Wally Tabor and I the greatest hunt of our lives."

Now I must admit I am more than slightly allergic to airplanes. I just don't enjoy myself in one. But before I knew what was happening

10

to me Croil Hunter had booked us on Northwest Airlines to New York, Pan American to London, and Air France to Paris, Rome and Nairobi.

We had almost a complete arsenal with us, including the new Model 70 Winchester .458 which Spencer Olin of the Winchester Arms dynasty had given me. Russ Aitken, the big game hunter, had warned me to take my shotgun along for bird shooting. Africa offers some of the sportiest upland game shooting in the world, he told me. But it is neglected by the average safari.

In New York, before our takeoff, Spence Olin and Homer Clark, the world champion live pigeon shooter, gave us a farewell party at the Roosevelt hotel. So when we boarded the plane I was ready to sleep through the ocean crossing. My airplane allergy scarcely bothered me at all. When I woke up, we had arrived in London.

We had a few hours wait between planes, so I used the time to visit Robert Churchill, the famous London gunmaker whom I had known since 1952. He confirmed Russ Aitken's advice on the Wing-master.

"You'll get a bigger kick out of shooting sand grouse than you'll get out of shooting a lion," he said.

At the Nairobi airport we were met by Ian Athow, one of Bowker-Douglass' white hunters. Ian, like Pat Hemingway, was a dedicated man. He, too, had fallen in love with Africa on his very first hunting trip there after being discharged from the Australian army at the end of World War II. So he simply stayed on, and became a white hunter. It was a living and a good way of life. Tall, spare and quiet, he had a craggy face adorned by the inevitable mustache you see on so many Aussies.

We checked in at the famous Stanley hotel, safari headquarters of the world, and were at once caught up in the excitement of the African scene. At the bar British accents and British beards were everywhere. To me the tone was familiar and nostalgic, for I had long associated with the British during my stretch in the Canadian army in World War I. But that night, at the hotel's floor show, I was struck by the incongruity of turbaned Moslems, straight-backed British, jeweled dowagers and retired Indian officers all mingling together.

The next day we piled into one of Bowker-Douglass' cars and started the five-hour auto journey to Arusha in Tanganyika. This was to be our safari take-off point. On the way we got our first close-up and fascinating glimpses of Africa—giraffes, a few lions, wild dogs, hordes of Thompson's and Grant's gazelles, zebras, wildebeest, ostriches, elands, dik-diks. Athow, incidentally, holds the world record for dik-dik, a small African antelope no larger than a small dog.

Lions are usually peaceful if you leave them alone. But as my friend Leslie Simpson, greatest of lion hunters used to say, "Never trust a lioness." Ray Hickock snaps this unusual pride of lionesses near our camp at Endulen, on the edge of the Serangeti plains.

We pitched our base camp under the huge acacias close by a cool, clear stream.

We soon found out that Africa not only had big game, but offered some of the finest small game shooting in the world. Hassein, an excellent cook, served breasts of guinea hen and broiled francolins. Although larger, the francolins reminded me of our native partridge. Their white meat was delicious. Pictured are the author, Hart and Jack Dow.

Most of the country between Nairobi and Arusha is a wildlife preserve, and game here is unmolested. Dr. Elmer Rusten, back in Minneapolis, had often told me that this was a photographer's dream. Getting closeups of the "dangerous game" is easy and completely safe for the shutter bugs. After long association with humans, lions will eat out of your hand. This is a fact few photographers bother to tell the folks back home when they recount how they risked their lives "to get this one." Another highlight of the Nairobi-Arusha jaunt developed when we stopped to view the wire-enclosed Mau Mau prison compound. This Mau Mau trouble is by no means a dead issue—yet.

By the time we got to Arusha we had worked ourselves into a lather of excitement. We scarcely noticed the forbidding dominance of snow-tipped, 19,500-foot Mt. Kilimanjaro some miles off to the northeast, nor the lesser, forested heights of Mt. Meru near at hand to the north. Pat and Ian set about collecting the equipment, while Douglass arranged for the licenses—a general hunting permit for each of us and extra licenses for the man-killers we planned to take. I took out a special lion license. Dow wanted a Cape buffalo and Hart was bent on shooting himself a leopard and a buffalo.

During the procedure of buying licenses in Arusha, Russell Douglass, the safari owner, turned to Dow and Hickok.

"I wouldn't recommend taking out a lion license," he said. "Jimmy Robinson has already taken one, and since there are only four in your party the one license may be enough. You see, it is very possible we may not even get one lion, let alone two, as lion hunting in Africa today is very uncertain. It is possible to go out and get one or two very quickly, but then again I've seen numerous occasions when we will be out five or six weeks with a party of four and come back empty handed."

Then, noting the expressions of disappointment on both Dow and Hickok, he quickly added, "Remember, not only is hunting lions quite dangerous, but you can waste a lot of time in the process and have nothing to show for it. You'll get plenty of thrills from the many other animals in Africa, and get much more hunting in if you don't have to take the time that lion hunting usually requires."

Both Jack and Ray looked at each other; then Jack spoke up "Well, let Ray take out a lion license and hope we can fill it. The lion is one of Africa's greatest prizes, a real trophy, and we have come a

14

long way. We'd be very disappointed if we didn't at least try for one."

Russell finally agreed to the additional lion license and it was decided then that the first chance should be given to Ray Hickok.

I was impressed by Pat Hemingway, a solidly built man with an ever-ready smile and an unruly lock of dark hair which persisted in falling into one eye. He was quiet, patient, sure of himself and from his own experience and his extensive library he had gained much knowledge of the game birds of Africa. His gun bearer, Mumbo, was almost as impressive—a 65-year-old native still as springy as an impala and equally quiet and sure. The whole side of his left arm bore the scars of an encounter with a charging lion long years ago. Before that he had fought with the British in World War I.

"Now don't get the idea this lion business is a pushover," Hemingway warned. "Just because you saw 'em lying around like overgrown house cats between here and Nairobi doesn't mean they're going to walk up and rub their backs against you when you're in the bush."

We were three truckloads heading out of Arusha for the vast Serengeti Plains, 6,000 square miles of Africa populated by four million game animals. Douglass decided at the last minute to go with us. Who could know Africa better than he? His own father had entertained no less a hunting guest than Teddy Roosevelt in the days when most of Africa was just a myth.

Douglass packed Jack Dow and Ray Hickok into the Beford truck he was driving, while Pat followed in his British Land Rover with Hart and myself. Leading the safari was a still larger two-ton truck driven by Athew. He had it packed to the gunwales with tents, beds, chairs, stoves, grub for fourteen days, sleeping bags, mosquito netting, gun bearers and trackers, skinners, the cook, his assistants and servants. In all, there were seven whites and fourteen natives from tribes called Wambulu, Warangi, Wameru and Monuwoze.

Mtu-Wa-Mou, a tiny native village on the River of Mosquitoes from which it is named, was our first night's stop. Then we moved on to Lake Manyara, a soda lake flanked by banana plantations along the famous Rift, where a good share of Africa's 2,000 species of wild birds may be seen.

"The boys in Havana tell me you are something of a wing shot," said Pat. "Suppose you shoot us a few sand grouse for the table. Also francolins, if you fancy white meat."

It so happened our first encounter was with francolins, a partridge-like bird, but considerably larger and just as dumb. There are more than a hundred sub-species and it is East Africa's commonest game bird. An old cock will weigh up to two pounds. Both sexes are all white meat, right down to the knees. Like pheasants, they have a strong disinclination to fly until harried by drivers two or three times. They fancy low thornbush and grasslands and they will sit like a pheasant and let you walk by.

"Here's the usual way to hunt franks," Pat Hemingway said. "You must herd them through the star-grass glades. They will run ahead of you, so you steer them toward the low thornbush patches where a beater can go in and flush them."

On the first francolin expedition I had Hickok with me who is a camera bug with a battery of boxes, and Dow, who had rented a fine 20-bore double in Arusha. Also Mumbo, the gun bearer. We walked up a bunch of franks and they scurried into a clump of thorn. Hickok and I stayed outside and upwind while Dow and Mumbo went in, beating the bush with sticks.

We could hear their harsh, rasping cackles as they took wing and came bursting out of the bush, one and two at a time, but in all directions like quail. They gave me some excellent side and angle shots.

The whole thing was slightly incomprehensible to our natives. For them the only gun was a rifle, and then to use it only on big game, something that adds up to plenty of meat. When they wanted francolin they used traps, or drove the birds into nets.

We passed through the scattered huts of the Wambulu tribe and arrived at one of Africa's wonder spots, the Ngorongoro crater. It is twelve miles across, 2,000 feet deep and loaded with game. Here we stopped at Safari Lodge, run by Gee Gosney, manager of Tanganyika Park. Gee formerly was a game warden in the Kenya Game Department and shot elephants on game control work. That night we sat up late listening to exciting tales of his hunting experiences and to those of his friend Gordon Harvey, the game warden.

Harvey told us how the game department controlled elephants that were damaging crops. "We hunt them in the moonlight," he said. "We dig pits about the same size and depth as a coffin, and shoot them like you would shoot geese in Canada from a pit."

Then he talked about George Rushby, the famed Yorkshireman

who was a professional ivory hunter. Rushby, he said, had killed more than a thousand elephants, more than any other man. He shot them the year around and sold the ivory at London auctions once a year. In his hunting days he made over $200,000 on ivory, but he is now a retired tea grower in Tanganyika.

We pitched our camp under a huge acacia tree the following night, near a little stream that flowed not far from the native village of Enderlin, west of the crater. This was a beautiful spot so aptly described in Papa Hemingway's book, "Green Hills of Africa."

It was mid-January, summer in Africa, and Enderlin was experiencing what would have been perfect July weather in Canada—50 degrees at night and not more than 80 in the daytime. The 6,000-foot elevation of Enderlin gave us an impressive view of the Serengeti Plains stretching away to the north and west. and on the east a towering range of mountains closed in upon us. This was lion, rhino and leopard country—indescribably beautiful and orchard-like.

I'll never forget my first day on the Serengeti. As I gazed out on the vast and mysterious expanse of plain, I thought, "Somewhere, out there, my lion is waiting for me. How soon will I meet him, and how will I fare when the moment of decision is before me?"

Pat rounded up Mumbo and Hassein, our skinner with thirty years of experience, and started out onto the thornbush-dotted plain with George Hart and I in tow.

"You'll have trouble with the light in Africa at first," Pat remarked. "It's deceiving until you get used to it and it may throw your sighting off. So we'd better start off with something big first, something like that wildebeest standing over there."

Pat was right. My former Canadian army sniping experience and Rocky mountain big game hunting was of no help to me. I had trouble with my first shot and finally realized that I couldn't believe my eyes. Maybe if I'd thrown my hat into the air, I couldn't have hit that either. Finally, my third shot brought down the wildebeest, a big, ugly creature that reminded me of a buffalo hunt I had with Captain Billy Fawcett on Clarence Parker's ranch in North Dakota years ago.

Mumbo and Hassein loaded the huge carcass into the truck. So we had bait for the lions. But camp meat was necessary, too, so George shot a Grant's gazelle and later I dropped a big eland, he with the horns twisted like a corkscrew.

Ray Hickock and his Kongoni. They are funny looking fellows.

Safari Lodge, located at the edge of Nogorongoro crater, one of Africa's wonder spots. Loaded with game, the crater is twelve miles across and 2,000 feet deep.

Pat Hemingway cleans the guns. Guns have to be in good condition for dangerous game.

The plain, in all directions, was dappled with game—herds of zebras by the thousands, wildebeest, the sleek, graceful and speedy Grant's gazelles, the smaller Thompson's gazelles and even ostriches. I was wishing Dr. John Moe could have taken out time from his surgery back in Minneapolis and joined us here. He would have plenty of subjects for his movie camera.

We needed more bait for Simba, the lion. George got it with one .300 Weatherbee slug—a fat zebra mare. Pat tied it to the Land Rover and we dragged the carcass two miles to an acacia tree near some low bushes.

"It'll draw hyenas," he said. "We'll get here at daybreak and if we're lucky you should have your lion."

Before the natives had finished wiring the zebra to the tree, so lions couldn't drag it away, the first scavenger appeared. It was Fisi, the hyena. A huge, wolf-like brute with hump shoulders, sloping spine, a shuffling gait and massive jaws. He sat on the plain, pointed his nose skyward, and there issued from his slobbering jowls the most unearthly howl I have ever heard, a spine-tingling loo-e-e-e, rising sharply at the end. Fisi was telling his pals to come to the feast.

Pat told the natives to gather some thornbush to cover the bait. It would at least slow up the hyenas so there'd be something left when the lord of the plains arrived during the night. Now we heard answering yelps from other hyenas and I could stand this ghoulish symphony no longer. Merely to look at this foul beast filled me with nausea and revulsion. I remembered Pat's casual words, "His jaws are so powerful he can snap through the thigh bone of a zebra as big as a horse, and that's something not even a lion can do."

I unslung my 30-06 and sent a bullet through this demoniacal thing. He rolled over once, then started dragging himself away with his inwards trailing. Then he turned and—I swear this is true—he began eating his own insides, taking huge bites in completely savage frenzy. I had heard that hyenas will do this when the smell of blood is strong in their nostrils and feeding madness is upon them. Now I had seen it with my own eyes.

Back at camp we were treated to hot baths in a canvas tub in the back room of our tent. Hart bought a slinking scrub dog from a nearby Masai, and Pat put it up in the fork of a distant acacia as leopard bait. Before dusk Hart and Pat went out to wait for the leopard in a boma the natives had built of thornbush. I got the details when they returned a few hours later.

"You know a dog is the leopard's favorite dish," said Pat. "So we figured we wouldn't have long to wait. Well, just at dusk I saw this leopard at the base of the acacia. He just appeared out of nowhere and was lying there. I pointed him out to Hart, but for a long time George couldn't see anything."

George took over the account. "Then I made out the head of the leopard. I was just getting ready to shoot when it disappeared. We waited some more. Pat nudged me. All I could see in the darkness was a kind of whitish spot. This wasn't what I was looking for, I thought. Pat whispered, 'It's him.' Before I could get the gun up the spot was gone."

"You see," said Pat, "the white was the leopard's light belly as he raised up to climb the tree after the dog. My whisper spooked him."

Back at camp that night, Russell spoke out, "This is the greatest lion country in the world today, and in my opinion if there's any place lions can be found it will be here. But don't forget, hunting lions is not an easy thing. They're extremely wary, magnificent hunters themselves, and their sense of smell is uncanny. Also, they're fearless and unpredictable.

"Remember, you must not kill a lioness, for it is against the law. You must take a male only. And it is extremely dangerous to shoot at a lion until you are very close, then only when you have a good, clean shot. There is nothing worse than a wounded lion."

With that Ray, Jack and Russell went out on the plain to shoot a zebra. They located a herd and crept up on it to within a hundred yards. Then Ray brought a fine stallion down with one shot. Their Mohammedan Masai guide bled the animal, chained it to the truck and Russell drove the Bedford over a circular route of about a mile to a cluster of thornbush which would provide fairly good cover with open lanes permitting some visibility.

"Now we'll chain the zebra to that acacia tree over there," said Russell, pointing to a single tree which stood alone on the plain. Within twenty minutes the native boys had the carcass chained to the tree and piled high with thornbush to completely cover it.

"That thornbush will keep the hyenas, jackals and vultures from getting at the kill," Russell explained. "You wouldn't believe it, but a lion can come up to this tightly packed and interlaced thornbush and clear it away in a few minutes."

It truly was unbelievable, because when piled high and tightly packed, these branches, with thorns from an inch and a half to three inches long, clung together in a seemingly impenetrable web. It would have been impossible for any human to have cleared them away without thick leather gloves and a rake. With the bait task finished, the hunters climbed back into the truck, but before Russell could get it started the hyenas, jackals and vultures began congregating around the bait tree.

"Don't worry about them," said Russell. "They'll just sit there and hope for the best. They can't possibly get past that barricade of thorns."

As they approached their camp, where they had left off a native boy to set it up, they saw the boy running out with his arms waving wildly.

"Simba! Simba!" he was shouting. Then he explained in Swahili that after the hunters had left him two lionesses had crept toward the campsite where he was standing. He promptly took to a tree and waited. The two big cats were still sitting patiently seventy-five yards from the pile of camp gear.

Jack and Ray were amazed to see Russell head the truck directly for the lionesses. "As long as we are in the truck it's safe," he said. "They will neither see you nor smell you." Then his hunters had the fantastic experience of approaching to within five feet of the cats so that they could have reached out and touched them.

These lionesses were to stay with that camp day and night and they gave the hunters no end of uneasiness and very little sleep. Even Russell was concerned. "They're up to something," he said. "We must be careful. Don't go away from camp and don't get too far away from your gun—ever. I've never known lions to act this way. When they stay any place this long they always have something in mind. They have no fear of campfires."

The next morning before the day's hunt got under way there was a very thorough inspection of guns. Russell explained all guns must be working perfectly, for if your gun jams, or you can't get the shot away, you may never get another chance and you may be even lucky to get away with your life. So it was two apprehensive hunters who followed Russell to the bait tree.

About two hundred yards from the tree Russell motioned for silence and whispered, "From here on pick each step so you don't snap a twig. Don't speak. When we get to that clump of thornbush be prepared for anything."

Fifty feet from the bait they peered out from the thornbush to see a beautiful, black-maned lion. But his head was up. He had neither seen nor smelled the hunters and he stared their way with his tail swishing in nervous tension. Russell gave Hickok the pre-arranged signal to shoot.

As Ray raised his gun, Russell's metal wristwatch band clicked against his belt buckle. The lion sprang into the air as though he had been sitting on a trap and then dashed into the thornbush. Ray followed his progress with gun raised, but no clear shot was offered and Russell immediately cautioned, "Don't shoot! Don't take any chances." Then he motioned to two rather unenthusiastic trackers and took up the trail of the lion. But after a hundred yards or so of tracking in the heavy bush, he decided it would be too dangerous to continue further.

A very unnerved, tired and hungry trio trekked back to camp for a belated breakfast and a council of war.

"There's not much use going back to that kill again for several hours," said Russell. "Let's take a couple of hours to do some practice shooting so we'll know what we're doing when we see our next lion."

He took an empty package of cigarettes and tacked it to a tree about fifty yards away. "Now let's see what you can do." He turned to Hickok. Shooting from a standing position Ray made the pack leap off the tree. We ran up to see what happened. "That's pretty good," Russell commented. "You were almost dead center. For a quick shot, that was excellent."

Dow cut the corner of the pack with the next shot, then hit it again on the edge. But Deadeye Hickok had two more clean scores on the pack.

"I guess we won't have to worry about getting our lion if we can find one and get a chance to shoot," said Russell. "Now I think we should find a new spot for bait. That last one was too low, a kind of saucer, and winds shift there more than they do out in the open. So we can go make another kill and set up a new bait."

Hickok felled an impala and again the hunters went through the process of dragging the carcass a mile or so, then chaining it to an acacia tree. The place was about sixty yards from an old Masai thorn-bush fence left from an abandoned village. After covering the bait with thorns, the group returned to camp for lunch. While they were eating they heard the roar of a lion. It seemed to come from the bait tree they had just left, and in spite of the fact this was more than a mile away, it sounded loud and close at hand.

"It's too much to hope for," said Russell, "but let's go back there and hope it's a male lion."

Three hundred yards from the bait Russell started a crouching approach, followed by Ray, with Jack forming the rear guard. After what seemed like an eternity they arrived at the old thornbush fence and raised up cautiously to look over its top. A nerve tingling sight greeted them.

There at the bait stood a magnificent black-maned lion and with him a beautiful lioness. The wind was favorable and they had not yet sensed the presence of the hunters. While the three men stood there transfixed, the lioness walked away from the kill. The heavily-maned male followed.

"The distance is longer than I like," whispered Russell, "but I guess we've got to chance it. Go ahead, Ray, but be careful because if we only wound him we could have some trouble."

Ray raised his .375 magnum, took careful aim and shot. The blast sounded like a clap of thunder. The lion sprang into the air as if he were reaching for the top branch of the bait tree and a mighty roar issued from his lungs.

"Good show," said Russell, calmly. "You hit him right in the heart."

But instead of rolling over dead, the stricken lion charged. The lioness, a little to his left, charged, too. For a moment both were lost from sight because of a dip in the ground.

Russell was genuinely alarmed. "Be ready! They're coming. Watch that lioness. She may come from the rear."

At that instant the lion came into view. Hickok shot again and scored another hit. Russell also hit with his shot, but Dow missed because of over-leading. Then Russell put a fourth shot in the animal, high on the shoulder.

24

"The lioness, watch the lioness!" he shouted. "Where is she?"

The lion, with the unbelievable impact of four shots in him, was still charging. For a moment he was again lost to view, but a yellow streak to his left indicated that the lioness was still charging too; although, confused by the shots and the actions of her mate, she was not in a true line for the hunters.

Now the big male came into sight again and at that moment he seemed to stumble, then fell and lay there on his side. A great wave of relief hit all three of the hunters. At least now they had only the lioness to worry about and the odds were becoming a little more favorable.

"Look in every direction," Russell ordered. "Keep watching. We're not out of this yet."

Hand shaking and with a parched throat, Dow followed the remarkably well-conditioned Russell and Hickok as they crept around the thornbush fence to see if they could locate the lioness. It was with a huge sigh of relief that they saw her streaking away. Apparently she had given up the charge.

"Good show," said Russell again. "Ray, that is one of the most satisfactory performances I have ever seen. You kept your head and did what was right and stayed with it. It was one of the finest exhibitions I have ever seen."

They approached the downed lion with extreme caution. "Keep your guns ready," Russell warned. "We're still not out of danger." He walked around to the rear of the lion so he would have a chance for a shot if the animal jumped. Then he gingerly poked the flank with his gun. There was no movement. He stepped back and looked at the other two men. "Well, I guess it's all over."

Back at the main camp Pat advised George and I to sleep with guns beside us as insurance against prowlers. I tried to sleep, but the lion I expected to bag in the morning kept prowling around my thoughts.

Long before daybreak, Pat, Hart, Mumbo, Hassein and I set out for the lion bait. Two miles away it lay just over the brow of a hill. I edged up to the summit on my elbows and stomach. There was no lion. Thirty hyenas were prowling around the bait. We knocked off two to scatter the rest. Then we headed back for camp. The scavengers of

Not an army, just our safari.

Pat and his gun bearer, Mumbo, are happy. Jimmy shot his lion—at the last minute.

George Hart takes a chance, but gets a picture of the lionesses at lunch—our bait.

the plains sat back in the bush giving vent to the maniacal gibbering they always express when thwarted by lion or man. It was the insane laughter of something out of its mind. On the way back I shot a dik-dik for camp meat.

Hart went out with Pat later to put up some more leopard bait— a stinking, three-day-old zebra carcass. Lions prefer their bait fresh, but leopards like it high, and this was a source of amazement to me. I simply couldn't reconcile the clean, streamlined beauty of this animal with his preference for carrion.

I spent the morning shooting guinea fowl for the table. Here was a tasty bird carrying a lot of meat. His entire plumage is black, spotted with white, much like our own guineas. The bird is highly gregarious and we often saw flocks of several dozen. Walter Wilderding, the famous big game hunter and painter, had told me about bunches of up to 2,000.

They love the semi-desert and scrub bush country, especially if white ants are prevalent. They roost in trees or tall bushes just before nightfall, and their droppings below these roosts always are telltale evidence of their presence in an area. When walked up they're a dull bird to shoot, for even in cover scarcely high enough to hide their bodies they will allow you to approach in range without flushing.

Once flushed, they always head for the nearest bush cover, so Mumbo and I worked out a sure-fire system to give me some sporty targets. When we spotted a "rasp" of guineas I would get over to the edge of the nearest thornbush and Mumbo would run in on the birds, flinging his arms wildly and shouting. They'd flush with an excited cackling and I'd get my shots as they came in. No. 6 loads did the job well, and no one in camp objected to the white, palatable meat, although it was a bit on the dry side.

While we were camped near Enderlin an old Masai warrior came into camp one day and reported he knew of a spot up in the mountains where there were quite a few rhinos. He readily agreed to go with us the next morning if we wished. I was still determined to get my lion, so Ray, Jack and Douglass took off about 4:30 the next morning with the Masai tracker, two gun bearers and a couple of natives who were bringing along supplies for the day.

For two or three miles they drove over a passable country trail. Then they came to the base of a very large foothill where the thick underbrush made further auto travel impossible. So they climbed out of the truck, gathered their guns and supplies and held a council of war. The pre-dawn sky was faintly greying in the east, so it was decided to wait a few minutes before plunging into the brush.

When the sky was finally light enough, a very beautiful and impressive sight greeted them. Mountains surrounded them on three sides and the thick vegetation had intermittent open spaces along a series of foothills that stretched away to the peaks.

"Stay close together," Russell cautioned. "Don't make any noise. Be prepared to shoot if a rhino charges, particularly when you approach a clump of bushes or any dense underbrush.

"It's a favorite trick of a rhino, when he hears or smells a human, to lie in wait for him. Then suddenly he will charge from what appears to be an impenetrable clump of brush. Often he will wait until you are only a few feet away. He will count on surprise and shock to enable him to reach you before you can do him any harm."

The little group had progressed only half a mile when the Masai tracker stopped, peered down and excitedly beckoned the rest to approach. He had just come onto a rhino track that appeared to be no more than an hour old.

"I'm not sure we should follow this trail," Russell said. "Maybe we had better cut around and come up on him against the wind. It would be a lot safer and lead us into less trouble."

After some excited discussion in Swahili, Russell decided to start tracking anyway and take a chance on trouble. Otherwise, the rhino might get away from the hunters and intercepting him ahead was a big gamble, too.

At this point one of the native gun bearers suddenly dropped behind. It didn't take Russell, Jack and Ray long to get their guns from the bearers. If the emergency arose, they wanted to be ready for it. The rhino they were tracking appeared to be headed for the top of the mountain. It was nearly three hours later and some 3,000 feet higher before they began to hit pay dirt.

Meanwhile, the journey was fraught with exciting moments. Frequently they jumped animals they never saw in the heavy underbrush. Several tense moments later they would learn from the tracks that they had flushed a reed buck or a wart hog or even a fleet cheetah, which can do sixty miles an hour in open stretch running.

The Masai tracker was an amazing character. Well in his seventies, he had the spring of a youth and seemed always to be running rather than walking on the trail. He kept going hour after hour without any appearance of fatigue. When we stopped occasionally to catch our breath for more climbing, he appeared to be very upset.

Suddenly the group arrived at a clearing that must have been about three hundred yards in diameter. Here the grass was shoulder high and the rhino's trail was clearly discernible as it led off to the left. At that moment, from the spoor, the hunters realized that they were trailing not one rhino, but two. They knew they were getting close because now they could hear chirps of the tick birds for the first time.

These birds are the rhino's watchmen. They ride on the animal's back, feeding on the ticks that infest the thick hide. But they earn their passage for two very good reasons; first, they solve the rhino's tick problem, and second, they are his alarm system. When anything approaches their host they set up a clatter that warns the rhino into alertness.

Apparently the rhino hasn't figured out that the tick birds also warn the tracker and alerts his hunter. The disturbance of tick birds always indicates where a rhino is and somewhat makes up for his advantage in the senses of smell and sound.

The tracker stopped and turned to Russell in excited tones. "He wants to know if we want to go on," said Russell. "He says there are two rhinos now and there may be three. If there are three, it will be bloody dangerous. One is bad enough, but three could really be too much trouble, especially if they all charged at once.

"Besides, we have only one license. Even if we successfully shot all three, I could get into a lot of trouble with the white hunter's association and with the government. There would be a very good chance that my license might be taken away from me."

Later Jack and Ray confided to me that if Douglass had decided at that moment to protect his license by turning back, the decision would not have been unwelcome to them. But Russell made a quick decision from which there was no turning back.

"We've come a long way," he said. "And I've been out many days without seeing one rhino on previous trips. We will keep on for a short while and hope those animals up ahead separate. If they don't separate shortly, I think we should get out of this as quickly as we can and take no more chances."

The party went on, another two hundred yards or so, to the end of the clearing. There the Masai held up his hand for silence. After listening a few moments, he excitedly broke into Swahili, addressing Russell. It was the first and only time on the safari that Russell turned white and looked downright frightened.

"We're really in a bloody mess now," he said to Dow and Hickok. "The worst I've ever been in. There aren't just three rhinos. There are nine of them. They have us surrounded and neither the Masai nor I know what to do. They may start charging at any moment."

Jack thought they should make a break for the trees at the edge of the clearing. Russell agreed, saying, "Follow me quickly and if they start charging we'll all form a circle and do the best we can." The entire group broke into a run and reached a cluster of trees, each about three or four feet in diameter.

"This is a bloody problem," said Russell. "I don't know just what to tell you to do now. We'll just have to wait and see. No doubt they'll start charging soon. When they do, keep your heads. Stay together, whatever you do."

He motioned to one of the gun bearers to climb a tree and point out the direction every time he heard a tick bird. The bearer had climbed only four or five feet when, from exactly behind them and not more than fifty feet away, there was an explosion like the sound of an automobile hitting a concrete pier.

The crashing sound came straight for the little group and a moment later Jack and Ray were confronted with the most imposing and frightening sight either of them had ever seen. A rhino was in full charge at them with the noise of a 40-car freight train traveling sixty miles an hour.

By pre-arranged agreement, Jack was supposed to shoot first, but it seemed like a lifetime had been lived before his shot rent the forest. Fortunately for the hunters, a strong 20-mile-an-hour wind was blowing crosswise to them, or the rhino would have gotten the first trophy. But the wind led him astray and his little pig eyes, with their poor vision, didn't help him to pick out the huddled group.

He missed the hunters by a scant ten feet and was twenty feet past them when Jack fired his first shot. The huge animal stumbled,

It pays to be cautious in rhino country. The tick birds are your only friends.

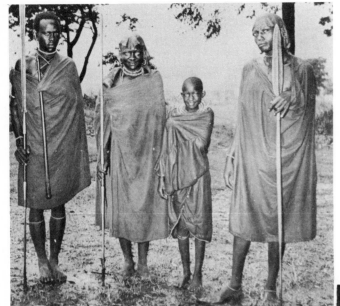

Masai warriors, Africa's lion hunting natives. They helped me find my lion.

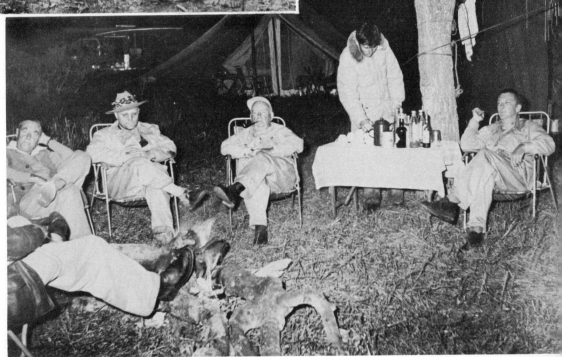

A disappointing day. No leopard for Hart, and no Rhino for Dow—only hot tea for Pat in the chilly evening.

then charged on for another thirty or forty feet before he dropped with a noise like a flatcar being dropped from fifty feet in the sky and hitting the earth. In the last thirty feet of that final dash Jack fired again and the .514s of Russell and Ray were speaking, too. All reloaded at once.

"Let's get out of here real quick," Russell said. "We'll go in the direction of that wounded rhino. Dangerous as that is, it's better than staying here where the others can charge us."

As he spoke another freight train charge came bearing down on the men, and a third behind the second. The hunters, tracker and gun bearers broke speed records getting out of range. Then, white-faced, they looked at each other and Russell finally broke the silence.

"This is the most dangerous situation you can get into in Africa," he said. "We can't go back. We must follow this wounded rhino, and he's unpredictable. Be prepared for a charge from any dense cover. They can hide in a few feet of growth. Sometimes they'll swing around and come at you from the rear.

"So, everyone be on the alert now. We must take our chances. If we're lucky we may get out of here. We may even find the rhino dead."

Then followed two hours of the most tense and difficult progress the hunters had made all day. Each clump of bush had to be tested with sticks and rocks before it could be passed, so that if a rhino were in there he would be flushed. The rear had to be watched constantly to be sure other rhinos were not trailing the party.

The hunters got half way down the mountain before anyone dared relax. Jack, wiping his brow, remarked, "Wow! I think I left ten or twelve pounds of weight up on that mountain. For a few moments there I wondered why I had ever come to Africa. Even Robinson's duck camp would have looked good."

Dusk was now approaching and Russell called the group together. "This is too dangerous to try and finish tonight," he said. "We'll go back to camp and come back in the morning. I know it is an unwritten law that no wounded animal be left to menace the countryside. But we can do no good in the darkness and it is a crime to needlessly risk human lives. Tomorrow we will finish the job."

Two hours later the three weary hunters were back at camp gorging a dinner of roast impala. They fell asleep wondering what the morning would hold for them.

It brought a happy ending. After another early start and a laborious trek up the mountain, they picked up the trail of the wounded rhino and found him dead.

Our camp was not far from Lake Eyasi, a few miles to the south, so when Pat and Hart returned from another leopard-baiting jaunt, we all jumped into the Landrover to have a gander at Eyasi. Here was one of the great lakes of Tanganyika, a haven for waterfowl of all descriptions.

"No doubt you'll see some teal," Pat said. "Maybe even geese, spur-wings or Egyptians. They like the natives' maize fields, especially when they're near water."

The lake was a 50-mile stretch of sparkling blue, nestled in 4,000-foot hills. As we approached it from the north, my eyes, accustomed to the flights winging off Canada's Lake Manitoba every fall, spotted a pair of big geese headed for one of the native's nearby maize fields. With Pat's Bushnells I watched them down and marvelled that our lorry wasn't spooking them. Then I remembered that these geese had probably never heard the report of a gun firing at them, so they had no reason for wariness that complicates our own American goose hunting.

The birds alighted on a knob of the field, not far from a patch of thornbush that would make a convenient hide. I suggested that Pat walk up a draw in the field, then run in on the birds and drive them over my natural blind. It was a perfect set-up, and it worked just as I had intended.

The big, amber-colored birds took alarm at the apparition of Pat running toward them and their whitish heads and necks stretched out as they clawed the air for altitude. They were so close I could see their pink legs neatly tucked back and their broad, white shoulder patches flashing in the sun. They were a pair of Egyptians, very beautiful and unlike anything I had ever seen before.

The lead goose crumbled at my first shot, and I took the second as it flared. Their six-pound-plus bodies hit the earth with successive muted thumps.

Pat retrieved the birds and brought them up to the car. "Well, you've got yourself a couple of geese. But maybe our boys will have to eat 'em. Egyptians aren't too tasty unless you get 'em young and cook 'em 'till they fall apart."

We went down to have a closer look at the lake and all of us thrilled at the variety of bird life we saw. There was a Goliath heron standing majestically nearby in the rushes and a pair of pied king-fishers swooping out over the deeper water. Pat pointed out a carmine bee eater, all vermilion and pink and blue, catching insects in mid-air. A flock of blackish African Pochards plopped down in the rushes, like the overgrown ducks they are, and several small bunches of tiny African teal whizzed past. Outstripping them for speed were the gar-graneys, a dull gray variation of the teal. There were shovelers and pintails and yellow-bills, the African version of our own mallards.

I hated to leave all this without at least bringing in a few brace of ducks, but we had no boat and no way of retrieving the birds. More-over, the day was waning and we had yet to put out more lion bait. I was beginning to think that maybe lions were a hex for me. So far I had been doing nothing but attract hyenas with my good zebra baits.

Hart had about given up on his leopard, so in the mornings that followed he joined me, visiting my baits for lion. We returned with plenty of minor stuff—an eland, ampala, wart hogs, Thompson's and Grant's gazelles—but not a shootable lion put in his appearance.

Occasionally we'd see two or three females at the sets, and once a young male, but more often we shot hyenas and wild dogs off the carcasses we left tied out for the big lion I wanted so badly.

I was getting apprehensive that I might wind up this Serengeti safari with nothing to show for my efforts. We were all a little edgy by now.

"Tell you what," Pat said that night. "Tomorrow we'll head off southwest toward the Semu river, and, Jimmy, I think you'll get your lion there. George may get a buffalo, too."

Hickok felt he'd done his bit, and he wanted some pictures. So he and Douglass elected to spend a few days at the Ngorongoro crater.

Pat, Hart, Dow, Athew, myself and two gun bearers started off for the Semu lion country. It was a brain-rattling trip over rocks and gullies through some fifty miles of the roughest country we had yet seen in the Rover. Several large eagles soared lazily above us, each capable of carrying a small antelope in their talons. The heat in the bush at 95 degrees was insufferable. All the tsetse flies in Africa seemed to be here. They were taking big hunks out of my face and I smeared myself with a special Donaldson's ointment that Hank Grossman had highly recommended for the skeeters. Hank may as well have given me vinegar. They licked up the ointment like Fisi does a zebra steak. Adding to our woes was the stifling cloud of dust that rose up from the plains beneath our tires.

But we forgot all this in an instant when I spotted something black in a dry creek gulch flanked by heavy thornbush. It was a Cape Buffalo. We snatched up our guns, clamored out of the lorry and rushed down to the creek bed. At the bottom of the vertically-walled gulch the tracks of a whole herd of buffaloes showed plainly. We started in pursuit, hoping the animals wouldn't double back on us, for then the gully would become a death trap. We'd be like ten pins in a bowling alley.

At the end of the draw we caught another glimpse of black in the dense underbrush.

I have always been known as a hunter with more luck than brains. This trip was no exception. I had seen the first rhino and could have bowled it over with ease, but we were in an awkward position if a charge developed. So I had to be satisfied with dry-pointing at the rhinos that stood stolidly no more than thirty yards off to one side.

Now, suddenly, I saw a huge buffalo with the biggest horns I had yet seen, standing quietly not thirty feet away from me. I whispered to Athow, "Better signal Pat to stop the caravan." Then I pointed out the big bull with my Winchester .458. It seemed obvious that Pat in the lead had not seen the buffalo. But I was wrong. Pat stopped and put his fingers to his lips, then shook his head as if to say, "Don't you dare shoot, you silly bugger."

Of course he had seen my buffalo, and a dozen more up ahead. Afterwards he told me that if I had shot, the herd would have stampeded and trampled us down like so many sheaves of wheat. Pat had, for some moments, been trying to maneuver us away from the buffaloes in a flanking movement. We were so close we could hear the animals breathing. But they must have heard us, too, for off they galloped. When we caught up with them again we could see there were at least three hundred buffaloes in the herd, not a dozen or so as we had originally thought. We were upwind of them, and this was decidedly no place to be. It was inviting a quick trip to the hereafter. Cautiously we moved around the herd some distance to get down wind.

Jack isn't our strong man. Africa's smallest antelope, the Dik-Dik weighs about twenty pounds.

Our guide, Pat Hemingway, and Russell—Bowker—Douglass, Ian Athew and our native guides. Pat's car is a British Land Rover.

A zebra, our lion bait, is chained to an acacia tree, then covered with thorns, so the hyaenas and lions cannot carry it away.

The herd was nervous and alert, but it didn't charge. Instead the animals began to move off away from us—all but a dozen that had drifted up against the wall of a bluff. Dow and Hart went in for a closer shot, with Pat covering for them.

"I had just about fifteen feet of vision," George said later. "There was this big bull about seventy-five yards ahead of me. It was now or never. I fired."

The bull reared up with a scream, crashed down and bolted off into the bush. Pat warned Hart not to follow. He and Athow took up the blood trail and found the wounded buffalo half a mile away. We heard their shots as they finished him off.

Our safari was nearing its end and I still had my lion to get. The animal had now become almost a symbol for me, a symbol of everything elusive, evasive and impossible. We set up a spike camp on the Semu and killed another zebra for bait and secured it to an acacia tree out on the plain. The next morning there was nothing at the bait, not even the hyenas and jackals.

"I was sure this move would produce something," Pat said disconsolately. "But then, you never know. Last trip out I hunted three weeks with a couple of chaps and we didn't even get a shot at a lion we'd want."

There was a small water hole on the plains about a mile from our spike camp. Pat suggested that since the sun had barely risen I might hike over to the water hole and try a few sandgrouse. It was an obvious attempt to get my mind off my disappointment.

"They'll come in for water about 7:00 or 7:30 and you'll have some of the prettiest shooting you ever got into," he said.

The sand grouse is a jet-propelled bird, something between a sandpiper and a pigeon but streamlined in the extreme. His plumage is yellow-buff to a chestnutty brown; his wings are long and pointed, and his flight is swift, swooping and spectacular.

They favor semi-desert country where the grasses are short and they thrive in countless numbers on the seeds of the grasses and bushes, desert acacias in particular. On bright mornings, after the sun has started its skyward arc, they appear out of nowhere in packs of a hundred to several thousand at their favorite water holes.

Pat advised me to take cover in some thornbush a hundred yards or so from the water hole. "It's better than standing close to the water.

They're not much afraid of a man, but the shots are too close. You'll get more sport on the flocks coming in from all directions."

The flight that morning was dramatic and unforgettable. At first I heard a faint peeping sound far away in the blue. Then I saw them, mere specks in the sky, coming fast in endless waves. In another moment they were upon me, flock after flock winging in from every quarter, banking in vertical turns, dipping and skimming the water, then soaring up again.

Pat had warned me to pick my bird or I'd draw no feathers. So, when one pack swept past me at thirty yards, I got on a center bird and pulled way ahead, firing as I led, in the hope that if I were too far out at least the leader might drop. The bird I aimed at folded, confirming my lead, and I had time to get another with my second shot. Immediately a new flock was upon me, and I dropped another pair out of this one.

There were some misses, too, when a pack would zig as I zagged, but in half an hour I managed to down two dozen birds. It was constant, sustained shooting. Still they kept coming. My gun barrel was so hot I had to quit. Never, in a lifetime of shooting, had I seen anything like this.

The thought of lions was completely erased from my mind as I walked back to camp. But that night, around the campfire, the old anxiety returned.

I fell to wondering if the trip was really worth it—$1,790 for the round-trip plane fare, Minneapolis to Nairobi and return, $850 per man for the 14-day safari, $300 for licenses, $35 for the conventional African safari outfits of shirts, trousers and bush jackets which you buy in Arusha—$2,875 in all. Norm Thompson in Portland had fitted George and I with Shikari hats.

"Well, we've got two more days," Pat said. "Tomorrow we'll just start out driving over the plains and see if we can find some lions."

I was ready before dawn. I'd come 8,000 miles for a lion and sixty or even a hundred more weren't going to stop me. We packed the spike camp outfit and started out. It was as cold as a winter morning off the Newfoundland coast. A 40-mile northeast wind was whipping up from the direction of the Indian Ocean. The temperature was 45 above. I had some long, heavy underwear that Mel Corrie gave me to try out and my warm Bob Allen parka never felt better. "I thought you told me Africa was warm," said Hart. "It's colder than the day you took Sam Bronstein and me on that wild goose chase down the Saskatchewan River."

By late afternoon we had traveled sixty miles in roughly a circular route, taking a terrific pounding on the rocky, gully-sliced plain. We were edgy, dusty and discouraged. It was time to make overnight camp.

Refreshed by a night of exhausted sleep, we were up at dawn the next day.

"We'll scour this country and maybe we'll run into a likely place to set out some bait," Pat said. "Tomorrow morning is our last chance, you know."

As we bounced along over the rugged terrain we came upon a

Left: Lions.

Below: Zebra and giraffes.

Masai camp with its typical cluster of cow dung huts surrounded by a boma of thornbush to keep out animal prowlers. George got out his movie camera and shot a hundred feet or so of film.

Some of the women were busy herding cattle nearby, others were drying out animal skins. And a few were engaged in preparing the typical Masai meal—the blood of their own cattle, drawn slowly and in small quantities so as not to kill the beast, an equal quantity of milk and finally urine, all stirred together. The Masai are not meat eaters and this concoction, revolting to the white imagination, is their sole diet.

The Masai children were playing with their dogs, lean, hungry, scrubby wretches whose miserable existence made me think of the

Above: Ostriches.

Upper Right: Cheetah.

Right: African wild buffalo.

striking contrast in America. I recalled the wonderfully sleek and finely trained dogs that Mike Crakes used to run at Fred Armstrong's dog trials back in Minneapolis. How Mike would have shuddered to look at these pitiful creatures.

Around the camp the Masai men were lolling in complete idleness. Tall, thin, daubed with war paint, each had his long spear beside him and its blade was honed to a razor-sharpness. His sole purpose in life seemed to be lion hunting. And he did this with only his spear. A Masai youth could not enter the realm of adulthood and be considered a warrior until he had killed a lion with his spear. Then he would be entitled to dress in a leopard cape or the mane of a lion, his sole adornment.

We learned from the women at this camp that Simba, the lion, had been working on their cattle. They went into hysterics when they described the beast that leaped over the boma and carried off one of their prize cows the night before.

With this news our hopes soared and we started out again to seek the trail. All day long we rode through the most rugged and rocky country I have ever seen. But not a sign of a lion nor even a track. We must have covered a hundred miles before we got back to our camp in the edge of the Serengeti. On the way back I shot a baboon and George downed a zebra to use for bait. These we dragged to acacia trees, fastened them with chains and covered them with thornbush to keep out the hyenas.

The vultures, obscenely impatient, came at once as they always do. Leaving my gun in the Rover, I walked to a nearby acacia to chase them away.

"Hey!" Pat shouted. "Don't do that! Never leave your gun in the lorry when you're out on foot. You never know what's in the bush."

While we were setting up the bait three Masai warriors had visited our camp and they were babbling excitedly with the cook when we arrived. Several hours before they had seen four lions in a clump of thornbush. Pat asked them to guide us to the spot and they jumped in the Land Rover to show us the way.

There they were, two females, the biggest I had yet seen in Africa. A quick chill raced along my spine as I looked at them sitting there, not fifty yards from where Pat had ordered me back to the car as I was shooing the vultures from our bait. What if they had decided to take me for bait? I wouldn't have had a chance.

44

George, his eyes glued to his camera as he ground out footage of the scene, remarked, "Here's a chance to get some good pictures for Paul Wendtland's Fur, Fin and Feather club back home."

The male, if there was one, kept himself hidden. But our Masai guides had sworn there was a male with the lionesses. Suddenly the bushes parted and another tawny beast sat down with the other two. Still no mane. The three sat there in the hot sun as unconcerned as preening housecats.

I had often heard that lions were as harmless as white-tail deer if you remained in your car and didn't approach too close. Then I remembered the tales that Leslie Simpson had told me years before. "Don't ever trust a lion," he said.

Simpson, a noted trapshooter, is still probably the greatest lion hunter of all time. He has killed 365 in one year. He first went to Africa some sixty years ago as a diamond mining engineer. Then, his fortune assured, he devoted thirty years to lion hunting and gave countless specimens of big game to museums. You'll see many of them today in San Francisco, Simpson's home town, and in Los Angeles.

I looked now from the lions to Pat's face for reassurance, just as I had often glanced at the face of one of Hal Carr's North Central Airlines' pilots on a trip into Canada's rugged country. If the face was composed I knew we were safe. But if I detected signs of concern I knew we were in for trouble. With Pat I couldn't be sure. I whispered to Mumbo to hand over my Remington pump shotgun and reached for some 0-0 buck loads. I've always had a lot of faith in this old stopper, and it once saved my life on a grizzly hunt.

If there was going to be trouble, I'd go down fighting. Past events raced through my mind and I recalled the time Axel Green of Winnipeg sat with me in a shell hole all day on the bloody Somme in World War I. Our insufficient refuge was out on no-man's land, and when the Huns had counter-attacked they came over us, spearing my friends with their bayonets like so many pickerel.

You would think that anyone who had taken part in a dozen or more midnight raids across no-man's land at Vimy Ridge would not quake at the sight of three mild-mannered cats fifty feet or so away. But I have to confess I have an excitable nature. If Africa had chipmunks and one had jumped out beside me then, I probably would have cut loose at it with the buckshot. My nerves were as taut as a violin string.

45

Hart and Pat, safe in the closed-in front seat, would have been of little help to me. If I didn't become too panicky, I might be able to get in a couple of shots. But what then? I remembered Jack Holliday, the famous big game hunter, telling me that he and his guide once poured seven shots into a charging lion before it dropped three feet from their guns. Now what if these apparently harmless cats decided we were unfriendly and made a dash for the car? They could streak down on us like lightning and we would be as defenseless as rats.

Then Pat started the Land Rover. He was going to look for the male, if there was one. "We'll just drive around that patch of thornbush over there and see if the old bugger will show up."

We drove slowly around the bushes; the lionesses paid absolutely no attention to us. They just sat there patiently waiting for us to be gone so they could get their dinner on our zebra bait seventy yards away. We completed the circuit of the thornbush without a glimpse of the male. So Pat headed the Land Rover for camp and we arrived just as the evening shadows were merging into darkness.

We had impala steak for dinner, with homemade bread and a delicious banana and pineapple salad that would rival the best I had ever tasted in Art Murray's famous steak house back in Minneapolis.

"That male will be there in the morning," Pat reassured me. "We'll go and get him then."

I am a sound sleeper, as a rule, but not this night. The chatter of birds had scarcely ceased when our lions started to roar out on the plain and the hideous hyena chorus joined in a crescendo of sound. I knew what was happening. The hyenas, caught prowling around the thornbush covering our bait, were being driven off by the lions. Soon the cats would take over and I wondered if they would still be there at sunrise and if the male would have joined them.

We lay there in our tents, side by side, listening to the uproar with only a single blanket separating us from the earth. It was Mumbo's turn to sit up for the night watch, and the little sounds of his movements outside were reassuring. With my belly full of impala steaks, I finally fell asleep and dreamed I was showing Hart's lion movies to a group of Minneapolis friends after feasting on one of Chuck Saunder's juicy tenderloin steaks at the Cafe Exceptionale where we have various game dinners.

46

The next thing I knew Mumbo was pulling the blankets from us. "Up, Simba waiting for you, Jimmy," he said.

Without waiting for breakfast, George and I gulped down hot coffee and climbed in Pat's Land Rover. In the faint light of early dawn he drove to within 500 yards of the bait, then he held a finger to his lips and motioned us to follow him. In single file we approached the bait, crouched at first, then crawling the last few yards.

The bait was gone. There were no lions. The only sign was some lion hair on the thorns we had piled on the bait, and these were scattered over the plain.

My heart sank. Now we must pack and get on our way back to Endulin, and then start home. There was Dow to pick up at the base camp and Hickok and Douglas at the crater. George sat in the front seat of the Land Rover with Pat and I climbed in back with Mumbo and Hassein. We started out, and I realized that now I'd had it. I didn't even care to look at the scenery.

Pat didn't head back to the camp. "We'll go a round-about way back to camp," he said. "We may run into our lions; their bellies are full and they'll want a little sleep," he added.

Suddenly my eye caught a flash of tawny color off to the left as we were passing a clump of thornbush. I shouted to Pat to stop, and then he took a look with his Bushnells.

"Holy smoke! There's your lion, Jimmy. Two of 'em."

We saw tens of thousands of Thomson's and the larger Grant's gazelles. A beautiful sight, reminded me of Wyoming antelope hunting. This is a curious Tommy, with horns nearly parallel and the under parts white.

The ugly wildebeest (gnu) with horns turned outward like a buffalo which may reach a maximum outside width of 32 inches. Both male and female have horns.

We often saw herds of several hundred Impala running and bounding high in the air. They are graceful and beautiful and have long, slender horns up to 32 inches.

They were sitting on their haunches on a mound in a recess of the bushes. We drove on to get behind the protection of the bushes, then got out and Pat, Hart and I crawled to within sixty yards of the pair. The wind was right and they had neither heard nor scented us.

Slowly, so as to avoid drawing attention with any eye-catching sudden movements, I raised up the .458 and put the front bead on the shoulder of the nearest and biggest lion. Then I held my breath and let off the shot.

The animal somersaulted in the air with a tremendous, throaty roar, then lay quivering on the ground. The other lion simply vanished. We walked up cautiously, guns at ready. Another shot in the neck did the beast in. So there, in the last possible moment, was my lion. "That's the biggest lion I ever saw," said Pat. The weight of days of anxiety was suddenly lifted from me. I felt as if I had walked into dazzling sunshine from a dark cave.

His mane was yellowish red and his shoulders were broad like Bob Tenner's. Hart was busy examining his big paws. "He's got feet like George Mikan," he said.

At Endulin we measured the prize—ten feet, three inches.

I'm satisfied now. Every hunter in Africa wants that first lion.

Next time I go to Africa it will be with a camera.

Like wolves, wild hunting dogs run in packs, destructive to game.

CHAPTER TWO

BULL CANS
of the DELTA

No bird, among all the ducks, fires the imagination quite so much as the big, silvery bull canvasbacks that tarry on the far reaches of Lake Winnipegosis until most of the other ducks are gone and the booming winds of October come hurtling down with the first bite of the advancing frost.

Then they arrow into the wind-bent canebrakes of the Delta marsh at the south end of Lake Manitoba and fall on your decoys like fiery meteors. They have come far; and they can dally but a short while for they have far to go across river and mountain to the eastern seaboard.

Lucky is the hunter whose time and convenience can put him on the Delta at the precise instant of the bull can arrivals. Most cans operate on schedule and pull out in mid-October. But these rare, big silver bulls are unpredictable. He who hunts them must be brave, too, and thoughtless of his own comfort because the wind will be bitter and the cold will penetrate to his marrow.

It was on the evening of such a day that I sat in our Sports Afield duck camp on the Delta, playing gin rummy with my old friend Walt Bush. Cec Browne and Tom Casey of Winnipeg were kibitzing. Wife Clara and Edith were busy closing up camp and Walt and I were the

51

only hunters in camp. Outside the clamor of the Arctic wind made us smugly content to be safely inside by a glowing stove and occasionally sampling the aroma of roast canvasback wafted in from the kitchen.

An unearthly medley of rattling and sputtering, climaxed by a terrible screech of brakes, rose above the thundering voice of the storm. Then it ended suddenly as it begun. Even the wind seemed still by comparison with the human juggernaut that burst through the door of our hunting shack. Walt Bush even dropped his gin-rummy hand to stare at the intruder.

It was Rod Ducharme, the giant, black-thatched French-Canadian from nearby St. Ambroise.

"Cheemy, da big bull seelver cans are here!" He had never learned to pronounce "Jimmy" like other people.

I had been getting ready to gin and this eruption threw me completely off my stride. "Will you drop?"

To Rod the game of gin was so much Greek. He probably never even heard me. "Yah, da bull seelver cans, Cheemy! De're here, ya betcha! In da mornin', by golly, we go get 'em, huh?"

I grinned, snatched a quick look at Bush's sour puss (he had been losing steadily), then I wiped the grin off and turned to Rod.

"What's here? I'm sleeping in the morning."

"Seelver cans, Cheemy. Da big bulls, I tol' ya about dem. Ya said t' be sure t' let ya know if dey come or ya break my neck. I come here fast as my truck go."

How Rod expected me to break his neck, set atop a 6-foot 3-inch frame carrying 280 pounds, I wouldn't know. But he seemed impressed. His skill as a Delta Marsh duck guide was as proverbial as his feats of strength, and they were legendary. Once, when my car was stuck in a heavy rain on a delta dirt road, Rod and his brother Louie had merely carried it to solid footing.

"You call that wreck a truck?" I said. "Sounds more like a wagon-load of loose bolts. And the only silver cans I know of are on the dump behind Hieberts' general store."

But I knew what he meant perfectly.

The year before, Rod had written me after we closed the duck camp. He told of being out on the marsh as it was freezing up and all other ducks were long gone. He saw some big flights coming in from the lake. They were cans—the biggest canvasbacks Rod had ever seen, and the whitest. They flashed in the sun like silver — "seelver cans."

I had at once put in a long-distance call to Bert Cartwright, chief naturalist for Ducks Unlimited at Winnipeg. "What do you know about overgrown canvasbacks that come into the Delta Marsh a week or two after most of the other ducks have gone?"

Bert had heard of them. He believed these outsize cans composed a flight from the most northerly part of the breeding range. Up there the long hours of daylight permitted them to develop more completely in body size and plumage. But few people had seen them. They came only after the big bays were making ice and the hunters had put their guns away. They stayed but briefly, then arrowed eastward for Chesapeake Bay.

"All right," I said to Rod. "Tomorrow it is—if I can get Bush away from this gin-rummy game."

Walt was skeptical. "Never heard of such flights before. I don't think they exist. But you'd have to break my leg to keep me off that marsh tomorrow."

At four the next morning Walt, Frank Lavalle and I were at Rod's house in St. Ambroise, thirty miles around the marsh to the east. Rod's wife, Rose, prepared a hearty breakfast of pancakes and home-smoked bacon.

"We take da truck t' da marsh," Rod announced. "Can't afford t' break down an' lose time gettin' dere dis mornin'."

I shuddered. Here was the world's most sublime optimism. What made this big meatball think his truck would hold together long enough to get us to the marsh?

Five minutes later were were careening madly along in "da truck," charging through an ice-slicked trail of matted cattails and cane. My fine breakfast was back in my mouth, my teeth were rattling and I was bouncing like a dowager on her first bronc ride. The morning was jet black and I couldn't see Walt, but at intervals I could hear low moans escape him.

Rod had two boats cached at the end of a narrow channel that extended inland from the Bay. They were frozen solid in ice. He and Frank went to work with axes.

We shivered in temperatures a few degrees below freezing as we waited. The north wind, raw and biting, was still with us, but instead

After dinner at the Sports Afield duck camp where the misses are forgotten and only the hits remembered.

Photo by Bill Robinson, Neepawa

Frank shouted, "Get set, Jim-my,—silver cans coming."

Photo by C. D. "Skinny" Schlesselman

of roaring as it did the day before, it was only muttering. This should be a good day for "da seelver cans."

We pushed the boats out onto the channel ice, then settled them through the crust, and Rod, in the lead boat with Frank, started be-laboring the ice with a bludgeon of an oar made from a 2 by 6 plank. Hercules, in all his twelve labors, never worked so hard. We made progress. Before I knew it, open water gleamed ahead through the now lightening gloom. While we were still in the ice, Bush changed to Rod's boat, Frank to mine.

We had almost a mile of open water to cross, straight into the bite of the north wind. Our destination was a group of small islands near the northwest shore of the bay. The silver cans should be rafted there, in the lee.

55

Dawn came as we were making the traverse, and the first ducks began to appear. A few goldeneyes, two or three tight little bunches of bluebills. There were no canvasbacks. The sky was clearing as the north wind pushed the overcast rapidly before it. Though I had on my long-johns, by the time we made the islands my teeth were chattering like a telegraph key, and I was bemoaning the ill-starred day I first met Rod Ducharme. That Jonah, with parka off and hands bare, had worked up a nice sweat.

He assigned Frank and me to a small island with a nice growth of bulrushes and moved on to select another shooting stand. The islands curved away to the southwest and Rod headed in this direction almost downwind. Soon he and Walt were out of sight behind another island.

Forty yards from our blind, Frank tossed out canvasback decoys—big, white-backed blocks for late-season shooting. He mixed a few "bill" stools with them. Then we pulled rushes around us, and I snuggled into a stack of hay with which Rod, in one of his lucid moments, had equipped the boat. The wind couldn't reach us here, and as the red ball of sun began to crawl above the wide marsh, the blood started moving in my veins again.

Still no cans. A few bluebills darted in and one flight of goldeneyes swept past. I thought nostalgically of some canvasback shoots I had known.

Now, the canvasback is the king of ducks in the old hunter's book, and an epicure's delight in the bargain. He is the hardest of them all to hit as he hurtles hell-bent across the sky. The big bulls remind you of a jet fighter with their bullet heads and sharp, small, swept-back wings. Those wings claw air at such a furious clip that they send the big, flat bodies racing along faster than any other duck. They are straightaway speedsters made for a big track, and they never flare or dodge.

One of the wariest of ducks and usually suspicious of decoys, once he has made up his mind, the canvasback just bores right in like a dive bomber on a pin-point mission. His reliance always is on his speed, and he is apt to get so close before you can let off a shot that he makes your 12-gauge pattern look like a rifle slug. When he comes tearing over you quail-high at 70 miles-an-hour air speed (often 90 in relation to you on the ground), you can take a bow if you drop him.

Somebody fetched me a clobber on the back, hard, and I heard Frank's voice shouting. "Cans, Jimmy! Silver cans. North. A big flight heading this way. Wake up, Jimmy! Get set."

I swiveled for a look behind me. A big flock was bearing down, riding the north wind like the tail of a comet. They were over us and past before I could reach for my gun. Then they zoomed up and wide, circled well out and parked in open water. Were they Rod's silver cans? I began scratching in the hay for my glasses.

"They were silver cans," Frank assured me. "I thought they'd never come. I thought they'd probably left the marsh. If you hadn't slept so sound I would have said to leave this spot an hour ago. Now I think we're all right. More goin' to come." He kept his eyes on the northern sky toward Lake Manitoba. The flight had come from there. I began tossing Rod's blasted hay overboard and at last found my Bushnell Glasses.

"They're comin'!" Frank said.

I saw a small cloud of dark specks which materialized almost instantly into a flock of cans—big ones—and they were heading straight for our blocks. They swept past, a long-shot high, and their great bodies flashed bright silver in the sun as I caught the quick whistle of their blurred wings. What music!

A few birds dipped a trifle; then they were over the bay. Frank gave them a brrr, brrr, and five silver cans sliced off in a tight bank. We hunched and tried to wish them in. Straightened out now, they came plummeting wide open to the blocks. I watched, mouth open. It was a sight to remember. Silver cans . . . big ones!

Somehow I got on the lead bird and pulled. It dropped, close in. Frank got it and handed it to me. I took it reverently. It was easily the biggest duck I had ever shot. And so white. I thought of Rod's description, flashing "seelver."

"More comin'!" Frank warned, and I hunched down. Three bunches were swooping in. They whooshed past and a dozen birds turned back to Frank's call. I took two big bulls and so did Frank. He marked where they drifted into the rushes.

They kept coming now, a dozen, five, three. They began to peel off regularly to the decoys, diving incredibly fast. We took only the biggest bulls.

"Hollywood was never like this," said Robert Taylor with a brace of Delta cans.

Photo by Maurice Smith, Winnipeg Free Press

"Never have I seen anything like this," Frank said. Nor had I. When he counted out our limit, we just sat there watching them in utter fascination. Several flocks were still slashing through the sky.

"Haven't heard no shootin' from Walt and Rod," Frank said, as we picked up the decoys. Now that I thought of it, I hadn't either. Could those two characters have missed the flight lane? We headed in the direction Rod had taken. The north wind was still blowing, tireless and raw.

Moving around a point, we beheld Walt. He was perched on a muskrat house swinging his arms to keep warm. Decoys were riding in front of his vacant blind, off to the right of the rat house. At intervals his arms would raise above his head and he would turn his face up to the heavens as if in supplication. It was positively mystifying.

As we got closer, I could make out a rapid-fire mumbling, then I was able to recognize a few phrases like "that no good" . . . "that bug-brain" . . . "that addlepated son of a . . ." This was not like Bush, who is the most mild-mannered of men.

"Is something wrong?" I asked soothingly as we came up. "Where's Rod?"

That did it. Walt seemed to explode like a balloon of bubble gum. "Don't ever mention that name to me again!" he roared. "I'm going to leave him here for crow bait! That's all he's good for."

He stopped to get a new grip on his vocabulary, "I've been sitting here on this ant hill of a muskrat house for hours . . . and that pea-brain's got my gun! He went away with it! I practically had to comb those silver cans out of my hair. I had to watch 'em playing in my decoys."

Another pause. "And what is he doing? Shooting silver cans all by himself. That's what he's doing. I heard a gun blasting all morning off in his direction—to the south. I tell you, it's more than a man can stand. Give me a gun. I'm going after that goatherder!"

I pushed quickly away from the rat house before Walt could climb aboard. My mind visualized a dozen possible contingencies— all bad. Here was a dilemma that had to be solved at once, without gunfire, and I was sure it would be much better if Bush was still enthroned on his muskrat pile when I came up with the doomed Rod. By this time, I reasoned, the rat house must be practically like home to Walt anyway. I closed my ears to his heart-rending cries.

I took an oar with Frank and we humped it downwind. Not far beyond Bush's throne, a considerable expanse of open water appeared with more islands on the far side. At another turn around an island, we saw a second figure on a rat house, also hysterically waving its arms.

"What goes on?" I groaned to Frank. "What is this strange affinity for Manitoba rat houses?"

It was Rod . . . who else?

"Start talking," I said as we edged into him. "You're in danger of having your hide shot as full of holes as a flour sieve."

Rod swallowed hard and rolled his eyes. His face wore a pitiful, pleading expression.

"Cheemy," he choked. "Cheemy, what have I deed? . . . Poor Walter . . . poor Walter! He want t' shoot dose beeg, seelver cans so bad!"

His agony was almost contagious. I think I felt a twinge of sorrow for him.

"I didn't mean it, Cheemy. Ya talk t' Walter. I am as eenocent as da new born babe. All at once, da oar she was gone . .. like dat! What could I do—sweem?"

Eventually we got his story. He had set Walt on a rat house while he put out decoys. In the process, one of his oars had slipped unnoticed from the boat and drifted out of sight. It was then he had discovered, to his total dismay, that he had Walt's gun. He had tried desperately with one oar to buck the north wind back across that stretch of open water, but it was no use. All he had been able to do was wait for the wind to die or for Frank and me to come. He had spent an anguished morning.

As he had crouched dejectedly on his own rat house, screened by rushes, the big silver cans had begun pitching into his blocks. It had come to be more than any mortal could endure. So he had taken an occasional shot as the morning wore on.

Rod pointed in his boat. Ten big silver cans lay there.

We tied his boat behind ours, and he and Frank pulled against the wind toward Bush's rat house. As we came up, Rod suddenly stowed his oar and became extremely busy with the decoys, untangling anchor lines. I looked for Walt's gun and couldn't find it. There was only one place it could be . . . under the boat's hay pile. If bad came to worse, Rod figured to have time to start swimming anyway.

By now Walt had taken in the situation and greeted us, relaxed, with a grin. He was still balanced safely, with the sure feet of long acquaintance, upon his mud pinnacle. But he must have had a bad moment when the good-hearted Rod raised his eyes for the first time and said:

"Ya look all in, Walter. I got a whole limit o' seelver cans. Why don't ya take dem and den ya won't have t' stay and shoot any more?"

Canvasbacks get hungry, too.

CHAPTER THREE

SPRING GOBBLERS

If Charlie Hay ever gets a new name in the hereafter, it will be Mr. Turkey. "Old Charlie," they called him around Montgomery, Alabama, and that was the only handle he responded to right up to his death. He made a living selling ammunition for Winchester, but this really was an excuse for him to get around the country where he could poke into every nook and cranny looking for turkey-hunting spots.

Wild turkeys were Old Charlie's passion, his reason for being alive in the first place, and the thing that spurred him on from one pine forest to another between calls on ammunition dealers. A typical Southerner, stocky, with an ever-present grin and an easy-going nature, the actual toil of peddling Winchester cartridges and shotgun hulls wasn't too difficult for him. Everybody loved "Old Charlie," from the farmer to the lumberman, and the city "feller" who occasionally came to hunt turkeys with him.

Naturally, Charlie attended as many Grand Americans. as he could up to his death. I remember seeing him at the big event, carrying his turkey call and dragging it out at the least provocation, just as the Stuttgart, Ark., duck hunters did who came to the Grand and rent the air with their constant duck calling. All that chatter "Old Charlie" haughtily disdained. His language was turkey talk.

One day he stopped at the press tent in Vandalia, Ohio, where I was pounding out newspaper copy about the Grand. He sat down and pulled out the turkey call, giving a few tentative squawks on it. Then he looked up earnestly at me.

"Jimmy," he said, "why don't you come down and hunt gobblers with me next spring? I know you've hunted turkeys on the King Ranch in Texas and with your friend Roger Crowe in Arkansas. But you haven't seen good turkey hunting. Come with me and the boys down in Alabama at Beatrice."

He paused to coax a few more yips out of his turkey call.

"Tell you what. Bring that George Hart feller that goes with you on so many trips. Come down for the March gobbler season and I'll show you how to separate the men from the boys in turkey hunting."

Now I'm always in the market for a good story. So I contacted my boss, Ted Kesting, Sports Afield editor. "Go ahead," he said. Back home in Minneapolis I got in touch with George Hart so I'd have a good driver. We rounded out the party with Herb Mueller, free-lance writer.

Two days of driving landed us at Montgomery and I soon saw that Alabama really has something to brag about when it comes to wild turkeys. There are few places left in America today where you can get an honest-to-goodness spring wild gobbler shoot. Just three states have spring gobbler seasons—Alabama, Arkansas and Mississippi. I had already hunted in the last two. I'd also hunted turkeys in Florida, Texas, Mexico and Pennsylvania. So hunting Alabama turkeys was to be a new experience.

"Old Charlie" met us at a Montgomery motel and soon had a coterie of his turkey-hunting friends gathered around. One of them was Jack Lovett, whom I had picked more times than I can count for my All-America trapshooting team. Another was Allen Rankin, Montgomery sports writer, who later did a story on our hunt for the Alabama Journal.

Next morning we visited the game department at the Capitol to buy our hunting licenses, and that added another hunter to our group.

"Take Kenneth Land along with you," said the game commissioner. "He'll take some good pictures and maybe show you a turkey or two." Land doubled as state photographer and game warden.

An hour's drive took us to one of the really unspoiled little towns left in America—Beatrice, Alabama. Lumber and turkeys are its main interests. Quaint and sleepy, it's still untouched by the march of progress. Charlie called it the "turkey capitol of the world."

The one landmark of Beatrice is a ramshackle, Civil War vintage hotel, originally painted white, you would guess, with its front steps sagging from the weight of the years. Its original owner had stated in his will that the hotel must be kept open until the doors fell off, and it looked like this might happen any week.

An amply constructed Negro woman called Nellie ran the place for the executors of the owner's estate, but she was nowhere to be seen.

"Oh, that's all right," said Charlie. "We'll just go in and pick some rooms and settle down. She only comes once a day to make the beds and collect the rent. If she isn't here when we go back to Montgomery, we'll just leave $2 a day for each man and put it on the desk. That's the way this place is run."

Nellie showed up before we were well settled and Charlie persuaded her to cook us a chicken dinner. It was delicious. We left a dollar apiece at the plate. "That's all she charges," Charlie explained.

He had invited "a few of the boys" over for the evening. About thirty locals showed up—everyone with a turkey call. I'd hunted often at Stuttgart and had to stuff my ears with cotton to get away from the continuous duck calling from morning to night. But this was the first time I had ever run into a group of turkey callers. They would spin a yarn, then argue about calls, then demonstrate their favorite yip, then settle back to add a new cloud of smoke to a room already so filled with tobacco smoke it was hard to see the man across from you.

Hart and Mueller were in their glory and they were learning a lot of things about turkeys they never knew before. Just one of their questions would call for an answer, then an argument, and then a whole flood of discussion.

The birds here, for instance, were of the eastern wild turkey strain, *Meleagris gallopava silvestris*, and they had long been the principal game bird of Alabama. In the early years of the 19th century they had ranged throughout the state in inexhaustible numbers. There were no game laws to protect them.

So the early settlers shot both hens and gobblers in unbelievable numbers as their staple source of food. They even trapped them and baited them. But it was not the toll of man, so much as his encroachment on their range by farming and logging, that finally decimated the huge flocks.

Phillip Henry Goose, in his "Letters from Alabama Natural History," mentions in 1859 the enormous numbers of wild turkeys. By 1890 a decline was noticed over the entire state and a decade later the situation had become critical. Still, it was not until 1907 that the Alabama legislature created a state game and fish commission. Then the first gobbler law in the United States was passed.

The law came almost, but not quite, too late. By 1940 the wild turkey population of Alabama was down to an estimated 13,500 birds. The game commission, of course, was working frantically to restore the birds to something like their former plentitude, insofar as available range would permit. It may be said to the commission's credit, the turkey flocks have been built back now to a population of 50,000 through careful management.

Turkeys are live-trapped in state sanctuaries and released in special management areas opened to hunting. Alabama now has both a spring and a fall season, with one bird a day allowed. The annual "take" is somewhere around 5,000 birds. Which is a lot of meat, considering that the wild turkey is the largest of all game birds, weighing around eighteen pounds. But some up to twenty-five pounds have been recorded.

To the backwoods folks of Alabama the turkey is almost sacred. A turkey hunter there is like our northern goose hunter—it's geese or nothing, turkey or nothing. There wasn't a man in our room at Beatrice that night who would have given two cents for a quail hunt, although quail are abundant in Alabama. When the turkey season opens, the town of Beatrice declares a legal holiday. Everything closes up until the season is over. Everyone big enough and strong enough to shoulder a gun is out hunting turkeys.

The pine-cone natives, whose lands the turkeys range, keep a careful eye out for their flocks, and woe betide the culprit who bags one of these kings of the forest out of season. But they would look with tolerance, and even disdain, upon the man who went out for quail.

When our gabfest broke up in the antiquated Beatrice hotel, Charlie announced that Dolly and A. D. Hines were to be our guides next day.

"Guess they're about the best two turkey hunters anywhere," he said. "They live right here off slash pine acreage they own, and they've hunted gobblers since they started cuttin' baby teeth. They know every turkey by his first name, and that's saying something, because they've got 5,000 acres of timber to hunt 'em in."

Through what little was left of the night I dreamed about turkeys. The woods were full of these rich, bronze aristocrats, with their bluish heads and pink legs standing out in distinct contrast to the dark green forest around them. They were all around me, but somehow I couldn't get my gun up to my shoulder to get a single shot off. It was too heavy.

"Hey! Wake up! You going to sleep all day?" Herb was shaking me. The time was 4 a.m. Before I could get my eyelids pried apart we were sitting in the little village cafe. It was crowded with hunters, most of whom we'd met the night before. They were all working turkey calls and arguing over where they were going to hunt. One group was going to Coon Creek, another to Slash Pine Valley. It was all Greek to me.

George Hart and I took off with Dolly and A. D. Hines for their farm. Charlie and Herb paired off with Bob and Francis Stallworth and were bound for another turkey "heaven." All of us were carrying 12-gauge shotguns and a pocket full of No. 4 shells.

"Couple of hulls is all you'll need, though," Charlie said.

I soon learned another reason, besides stocking, why turkeys are thriving in Alabama. Our four-wheel-drive jeep was puffing and sloshing back into the swampiest and thickest cover I had ever seen. There was water and mud and forest everywhere. Just as the sky was getting grey we reached our destination, four miles back in the swamp. There was bird chatter everywhere as the avian life awoke to the new morning, soft, mild and sixty above. A busy woodpecker drummed away on a nearby tree.

We climbed out of the jeep and Dolly put his hands to his mouth, emitting the "whoo-whoo-whoo" of an owl ready to settle down for his day's sleep.

An immediate answer came — from a turkey. "Gobble-gobble-gobble." It was off to the right. Then another came from the left.

"We'll take that one over there on the right," Dolly said, pointing. Then my long, lanky partner beckoned me to follow and we stepped out into the tangle, threading our way silently as Indians.

Grove Forster and Charlie Hay satisfied they'll keep in the freezer until Thanksgiving.

*Herb Mueller and Charlie Hay,
well hidden in a blind, awaiting
a gobbler.*

Photo by Kenneth Land

*George Hart, Jimmy,
A. D. Hines and Dol-
ly Hines negotiated
swampy and thick-
cover in the jeep.*

We progressed slowly about 400 yards before he stopped. Bending to my ear, he whispered, "We'll make a little blind right here."

It was constructed in a little ditch beside a faint path winding through the gloom. I knew then that he expected the gobbler to come right down the path to us. But I wondered about that owl call.

"Gobblers always investigate an owl call," he whispered.

Now he got out his turkey call, a hand-made box affair that he treated as though it were made of platinum. He issued a few short yips on it.

The response was prompt. This gobbler undoubtedly had already left his roost somewhere back there in the top of a tall pine tree. Now, step by slow step, he would come to see where this charming lady might be waiting for him. It was certain to be a lone gobbler, because flocks do not respond to calls. They expect a lone caller to come to them.

Dolly was using all the turkey psychology he knew, which was plenty. He let no more yips out of the box for a spell. Not only is the turkey the wariest and wisest of all game birds, but an old gobbler is the keenest of them all. When he hears his princess call, he will answer and come. But if the call is repeated too soon, he loses interest. The lady's silence is what intrigues him.

After an appropriate silence, Dolly permitted another yip to escape his box. The answer was closer now. That meant there could be no mistakes from here on. A false note in a call could be more readily detected now. And we must remain frozen into immobility, for a turkey has the eyes of an eagle. He'd notice a bumblebee moving at thirty yards.

I could picture this gobbler, advancing slowly, head erect, wary but curious, and a little eager to see the author of this call that came so tantalizingly at long intervals. He would be sure to notice any unusual piling up of brush, so Dolly had been careful to make our blind as inconspicuous as possible. And there we sat, side by side, as quiet as mice, immobile as rocks.

Now I could hear the turkey's footsteps as he approached on the path. They reminded me of a cow walking, and I knew this must be a heavy bird. Each step was separate—poised and spaced. My heart began to pound in my ears. The tension was almost too much to bear.

Then I saw him. His head bobbed from side to side as he searched for his lady love. Dolly nudged me and nodded, indicating now was the time.

I leaped to my feet. But my foot caught in an exposed root. Over I went, clawing the air. The startled gobbler exploded into action and was off.

Dolly just looked at me, sprawled out in front of the blind. And if looks could kill, I wouldn't be here today.

That was it. We combed the woods for the rest of the day, but couldn't get a gobbler answer anywhere. Later I learned that George had been equally unfortunate. His turkey was within forty yards of his blind when he couldn't repress a sneeze. Herb had seen a gobbler, but couldn't get it in range.

"Just seeing one of those big, bronze things is worth the trip, though," he remarked.

We ran into more hard luck the next day. I could heartily agree with Charlie Hay when he vowed that the turkey gobbler is the smartest thing alive, bar nothing. George, however, redeemed himself by bagging an 18-pounder.

At the Beatrice hotel we ran into a new group of hunters from Mississippi. They were on their annual trip to the area for turkeys. One proved to be an old friend, Hughie Critz, former second sacker for the Cincinnati Reds and the New York Giants. He had started his major league career in the American Association with Minneapolis.

"How are Dick Cullum and Charlie Johnson and Rollie Johnson?" Hughie wanted to know. "And Joe Hennessy and George Edmonds?"

These were sports writers I knew well in the Twin Cities. So the conversation turned from turkeys to baseball. Later we played poker with the newly arrived guests and I didn't get to bed until 2 a.m. So, on the following morning, I had Herb in my hair again.

"Did you come all the way to Alabama just to play poker?" he asked, pulling my bed covers off in the 4 a.m. darkness. "Or do you want me to go out and shoot your turkey for you?"

I groaned. "Just tell Dolly I got a splitting headache. Tell him to come back at noon and pick me up. Do we *have* to go out and wake those turkeys up?"

The next thing I knew Dolly tipped the bed over on me. I got up. A quick snack and we were back in the woods again, but I had no heart for it. I could scarcely keep my eyes open.

"Let me sit in that blind near the road today," I begged Dolly. "I don't think I could walk a step. But I'll be all right tomorrow."

There was a turkey blind about half a mile from the Hines farmhouse, and I had my plan all laid out. After Dolly had planted me in the blind, I would scoot back to the house and catch a few hours of sleep.

Dolly made some minor repairs to the blind, then prepared to take off into the woods. I sat with my back to the trunk of a pine and stared out at a little opening in front of me about a hundred yards square. The grass was knee high in the opening and a few scattered pines gave it a park-like effect.

"I'll head over to Possum Creek," Dolly said. "Be back about sundown. Just rest your bones here in this blind, but I don't think there's much of a chance for a turkey here."

Dolly hadn't been gone more than two minutes when I began to feel drowsy, with the sun shining brightly into my blind at the base of the pine tree. Before I knew it I was sound asleep.

What wakened me was my own shaking from a chill. I looked at my watch. It was 5 p.m. and the sun had gone down behind the trees. No wonder I was chilled. Then I came up with a start.

"Caw-caw-caw!" A big, black crow was dive bombing something out there in front of me. He would come zooming down, skim low over the grass, then circle upward and repeat the process, cawing angrily all the while. I shifted so I could get my gun to my shoulder.

"Well, maybe I won't get a turkey, but there'll be one less crow in Alabama," I told myself.

Just as I was levelling on the crow something more important caught my eye. It froze me in my tracks. There, not thirty yards in front of me, was the biggest wild gobbler I had ever seen. He saw me at the same time and took a few running steps, as turkeys do, to get airborne.

I let him have one blast of No. 4 shot. He crumbled to the ground, flopped a little in the grass and was stone dead when I ran up to him.

At that moment Dolly burst out of the timber to my right. One look at the huge gobbler I held up proudly stopped him in the middle of a step.

"Well, I'll be a snake-bit houn' dawg!" Words failed Dolly after that. He just stood and gawked.

"How much you think he'll weigh, Dolly?"

The lanky, old woodsman hefted the bird. "Hmmm-mm. Go a mite over eighteen pounds, I'd say."

Back at the hotel there was general jubilation. George Hart had bagged himself a second turkey and Herb Mueller had collected a big gobbler, too. But they admitted they must have covered fifteen miles to accomplish the feats.

"You guys are suckers," I said. "I didn't walk fifteen feet from the jeep to get this one. The idea is—you don't go to the turkey, you make the turkey come to you."

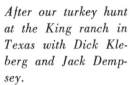

After our turkey hunt at the King ranch in Texas with Dick Kleberg and Jack Dempsey.

Nellie, our cook, promises turkey for dinner.

73

CHAPTER FOUR

Memories of Annie Oakley

Through all the pages of American history firearms have played a greater part than statesmen, Indians or the covered wagon. And if you studied that history closely it would reveal that no one was as adept with a gun as a little Ohio farm girl named Annie Oakley.

Before her death in 1926 at the age of 66, I knew Annie Oakley well. In fact, she left to me, along with Will Rogers and Fred Stone, several of her mementos of a life filled with adventure and glory. Long before her death her name was a legend in the shooting world.

The story of her life, as I learned about it from her own lips, reads like a novel. It began in the little Ohio hamlet of Woodland where she had been christened Annie Moses. Until recently, a brother, John Moses, still lived in nearby Greenville, Ohio, and I used to hear from him often.

Annie was the oldest of five children, and before she was out of her baby clothes her father died. Her Quaker mother had a bitter struggle to rear her brood. So Annie, before she had turned into her teens, had learned to supplement the family larder with game she shot in nearby woods and fields.

With her uncanny skill at shooting, she became the principal support of the Moses family while still a child. And it was shortly after she had turned fifteen that the biggest event of her life occurred.

A professional exhibition shooter for Remington Arms Co. was making a tour of the country. His name—Frank Butler. When he got off the train at Greenville to fill a shooting date he was blissfully ignorant of what lay in store for him. But he noticed an unusual hubbub among the farmers in town. Hotels were packed and space in rooming houses was at a premium.

Butler asked a couple of farmers on the street what it was all about.

"Why, we expect to have the time of our lives tomorrow," he said. "A feller named Butler is going to shoot against little Annie Moses. He'll get the surprise of his life."

Butler found himself feeling sorry for this little girl, whoever she might be. He, the great Frank Butler, pitted against a farm girl.

When he saw the pretty, curly-headed Annie next day at the packed gun club he was even a little amused. But the amusement soon turned to chagrin when Annie Moses beat the great Butler in a closely contested live pigeon shoot on fifty birds.

The Cincinnati Enquirer came out with screaming headlines, "Frank Butler Thinks He Can Shoot!" Butler now wasn't so sure. He had shooting dates way out to the west coast, but now who would want to see an exhibition by a shooter who had been defeated by a country girl?

Moodily he informed the factory of his defeat. A wire came back directing him to sign Annie up as a shooting partner. But the Remington bosses had reckoned without Mrs. Moses, Annie's mother. She decidedly was not in favor of her young daughter gadding about the country. All her Quaker religion rebelled against the idea.

Butler pleaded in vain, then wired the factory of his failure. Back came the directive: "Sign Annie or you're fired." Butler returned and painted a glowing picture for the obdurate mother. The family would be independently wealthy. It would gain social status.

But Mrs. Moses was staunch. It wasn't proper for young ladies to travel around the country, especially young Quaker ladies, if they were unattached. Butler failed to catch the broad hint. He resumed his pleas. Finally, the mother stopped him.

"Mr. Butler," she said, "Annie can't travel around the country with any show—except—unless—you marry her. Then she can go."

76

To Frank's credit and everlasting benefit, he rose to the occasion. He had not failed to note that Annie possessed charms. That same day he rushed her to a preacher and they were married. The marriage lasted until Annie's death. Frank died a month later.

The young couple joined the famous Buffalo Bill show in 1884 and traveled with this troupe for seventeen years. It was then that little Annie Moses acquired the name Annie Oakley, bestowed upon her by Buffalo Bill himself.

When Sitting Bull, the great Sioux Indian chief, saw Annie shoot in Minneapolis, he called her "Little Sure Shot." Later they became fast friends, and one of her most cherished possessions was a bow and arrow given her by Sitting Bull.

Throughout her travels with the Buffalo Bill show, Annie never tipped the scales at more than a hundred pounds. A year before her death at 66 she visited the Grand American trapshooting championships and broke 97 of 100 targets.

In her seventeen years with the show she traveled in fourteen countries, giving exhibitions during show vacation periods and hunting. She was entertained and given costly gifts by kings, queens and emperors. King Edward of England, then Prince of Wales, gave her a gold medal with the inscription: "You are the greatest shooter I ever saw, and America should be proud of you."

Often she used to recall to me how she had taught Sitting Bull how to read and write. Before his death he made her his heir and presented her with the headdress he wore in the battle with Custer.

One of Annie's greatest performances in this country took place on two successive days in 1888 at Gloucester and Trenton, N. J. At Gloucester sportsmen wagered $5,000 that she could not kill forty birds out of fifty at thirty-three yards. Annie killed forty-nine. These were fast live pigeons, used in those days in the big shooting matches. Next day at Trenton she shot with the famous Miles Johnson in a 50-bird race and defeated him before a crowd of 5,000.

Annie's hair turned white in the train wreck which ended the Buffalo Bill show and in which seventeen were killed. After her death she left a fortune estimated at half a million dollars.

When I used to see her and Frank Butler the two of them often told me that Buffalo Bill, despite his great build-up, was never a great shot, but he did build up a big reputation as a buffalo hunter.

They rated "Doc" W. F. Carver as the greatest rifle and shotgun marksman in the world at that time, and Wild Bill Hickock by far the best pistol shot. When I asked Annie how Carver got the nickname "Doc" she said it was because he was forever practicing medicine on wild animals and birds.

During the late 1890s there were many really great live pigeon shots in the country. Among the best was J. A. R. Elliott of Kansas City, uncle of Russ Elliott who now manages the Kansas City Gun Club. Others were Bill Crosby, the great O'Fallen, Ill., trapshooter and Tom Marshall, official scribe of trapshooting and the only man ever to win two Grand Americans on live pigeons—in 1897 and 1899.

Tom Marshall met Carver on two occasions in special matches, and each time Doc won by a small margin. In 1894 J. A. R. Elliott shot against Carver for the world championship on live pigeons at the Kansas City Gun Club and was beaten by just one bird when Doc killed 95 out of 100.

That same year Crosby took on Carver in a live pigeon race and won the first match, but lost the next two. Then, in 1901, my old friend Paul North, a target manufacturer from Cleveland, raised $4,000 to send an American team over to shoot against the British. The matches were staged at the Middlesex Gun Club in London. The Americans easily defeated the British and Bill Crosby was high scorer with 93 of 100.

Others on that team were J. A. R. Elliott, Charlie Budd, Ernie Trip, "Pop" Heikes, T. S. Parmalee, R. Merrill, Jack Fanning, Fred Gilbert and Tom Marshall. "Pop" was a native of Dayton, Ohio, and won the first Grand American handicap trapshooting championship in New York in 1900. He was a great shot and worked for me selling Sports Afield magazines up to his death.

After beating the British, the American team went on to Scotland and easily won there. Gilbert and Merrill each shot 100 straight birds and Crosby got 99.

In those days some great shots were developed because they practiced day in and day out on glass balls, live pigeons, clay targets and wild game. But I think our present-day shooters like Clyde Mitchell, Herschel Cheek, Cliff Doughman, Fred Waldock, Art Finney, Joe Devers and others could hold their own against the old-timers.

78

Joe Devers, now of Reno, Nevada, was placed on my Sports Afield All-American trapshooting team this year. In my estimation he is the greatest present all-around shot in the world at skeet, trap and on live pigeons. He's a natural 99 per cent shooter on both skeet and traps, and when I visited the live pigeon shoot at Monte Carlo a few years back they told me Devers was the best all-around pigeon shot in Europe.

While I used to do considerable shotgun shooting on game as a farm boy on the southern Manitoba prairie, my first real experience with a rifle didn't come until I went across to France with the 44th Canadian Infantry in World War I. I had enlisted at Sewell Camp in Manitoba early in 1915 when I was seventeen.

I served as a rifleman, machine gunner, sniper and gas sergeant during the battles of Ypres, the bloody Somme, Vimy Ridge, Paschendale and other fronts. Our unit was known as the "Suicide Battalion." During the Regina trench battle at the Somme in October, 1916, we lost 500 of our 850 first-line soldiers when we attacked the Huns without a barrage.

After the war I played hockey and baseball in Manitoba and North Dakota for three years. Then I migrated to Chicago where I hooked up with the Amateur Trapshooting Association, a job that fitted in perfectly with my earlier experience. I attended my first Grand American at Chicago in 1923, then moved to Dayton, Ohio, where the trapshooters built their own permanent home and where the Grand American is held each year now.

At Dayton I handled publicity for the big event, which now has grown into a spectacle featuring more than 2,000 gunners from all parts of the world for ten days of firing. There, in those early Grand Americans, I had the good fortune to meet many of the old timers who had been shooting in the late 1890s when Annie Oakley was at her peak. From these old shooters I got many interesting tales of their market hunting experiences and shooting feats.

In 1925, while at Dayton, I started writing for Sports Afield. It was then that I got well acquainted with such shooting greats as Ad and "Pinkie" Topperwein, Fred Gilbert, "Pop" Heikes, Charlie "Sparrow" Young and others. From them, particularly Pop and Annie, I learned much more about the old time shooters. What these two didn't fill me in on, Charlie Young did. He, too, was one of the greats, having shot

Annie Oakley

The live pigeon shoot at Monte Carlo—Shirley Devers, Victor de Borman, Joe Devers, Ralph de Leon, Jim Naegele and Sandor Dora.

Photo by Robert Churchill

Watching the famous Grand Prix live pigeon championships at Monte Carlo—Count de Teba, Ben Gallagher, the author, and Edward LeFebure Despeaux. The Monte Carlo pigeon grounds are directly in front of the Casino on the blue Mediterranian.

Photo by Geo. Hart

in all the Grand Americans from 1900 up to a few years ago when he passed away at eighty.

These old timers were full of shooting anecdotes and I acquired from them a knowledge that was invaluable to me in later years. I have often felt that I was very lucky to reap so much information. I am forever grateful for having had the opportunity.

I had long yearned to make a trip back to Europe and visit the old battlefields, attend the live pigeon shoots and meet the famous gunmakers. So, in 1952, George Hart of Minneapolis and I packed our guns and set sail for Europe. Our first stop was at Monte Carlo where we attended the Grand Prix pigeon championships.

The fabulous Monte Carlo shooting grounds, located directly in front of the Casino, was the scene of the first Grand Prix live pigeon shoot in 1872. George Lorillard, the New York tobacco magnate, won that year. Ted Renfro of Armstead, Montana, was the next American to win the big event. That was in 1931. Two years later Walter Warren of Milwaukee won it, and in 1951 Tony Banchero of San Francisco was the winner.

When George Hart and I visited Monte Carlo our own American shooter, Joe Devers, was top pigeon shot in Europe. But he didn't win the Grand Prix, although he was high-over-all for the 60-day meet. His wife won the Grand Prix ladies' championship, one of the most colorful live pigeon competitions in Europe.

We met Count Teba of Madrid, Spain, one of the world's greatest game shots and holder of the European long run record of 112 straight zuritos, the tricky Spanish live pigeons. We met Dora Sandor, the Austrian gunner and winner of the Grand Prix in 1931 and 1932. We visited with Robert Churchill in London, getting well acquainted with this famous gun maker and author of the book, "Game Shooting."

We chatted with Ben Gallagher, formerly of Omaha and now living in Paris, and with Manfredi Adolfo of Bologna, Italy, a famous munitions manufacturer. Then we visited the famous San Remo Gun Club in Italy with Joe Devers and found it intensely interesting.

There were others equally unique. Walkup shooting was featured at the Villebob-Meuden Club in Paris. And the Bois de Boulonge Club, in downtown Paris, is one of the most beautiful clubs in the world. Here they shoot skeet, live pigeons and traps over a small lake.

82

Another famous club was the Le Faisceau, owned by Gene Renette of the firm of Gastine-Renette, French gunmakers for years. Gastine owns a fine sporting goods store in Paris and I had visited it many times during my numerous trips to Paris in World War I. The 1924 Olympic trapshooting championships were held at Le Faisceau and on the American team were Fred Etchen as captain, Billy Fawcett as manager, Frank Hughes, Bill Silkworth, Sam Sharman, Clarence Platt and Johnny Noel. I had the honor of helping pick this team.

Incidentally, American teams have shot in three Olympic competitions—1912 at Stockholm, 1920 at Antwerp and 1924 in Paris. On each occasion the Americans won.

At Le Faisceau Club Hart and I met and shot with many famous sportsmen, including Prince Achille Murat, Madame Pigeon, Guy Jaques, famous gun writer, M. and Mme. Jean Pierre Guerlain, the

Robert Churchill of London, England, famous gunmaker and author of the book "Game Shooting."

83

Ad and Plinkey Topperwein, two of the most famous and widely-known exhibition shooters of all times.

Ken Beegle, the famous exhibition shooter, draws an Indian head while wife Blanche watches.

Photo by Jack Mitchell

Forest Saunders does exhibition shooting with shotgun and rifle at gun clubs, fairs and sportsmens shows. Here he demonstrates the proper stance for doubles trapshooting.

Photo by Bob Ehlin

ing Bull, who traveled with ffalo Bill's show for many rs, nicknamed Annie Oak- "Little Sure Shot," after ing her shoot in St. Paul.

Exhibition shooter Herb Parsons, who can throw seven clay targets in the air with his left hand, then breaks them all with his pump gun before they reach the ground.

perfume magnates, Bruno and Ed Lefebvre-Despeaux, who own one of the best shooting preserves in France, and Count de Salverte, who has one of the finest castles in Europe, and Jack Meyer of the famed St. Hubert Sporting Goods Store. The count invited us for a hunt, which time prevented us from making.

On our return to America, refreshed by the places we had seen and the people we had met, I turned enthusiastically to renewing my acquaintance with the history of trapshooting, which was born in England in 1793. It was called "popinjay" then, indulged in by bow and arrow marksmen for practice upon flying and moving game.

The first trapshooting club was formed in 1810 at the Hornsey Wood House Pigeon Club in England. The earliest record of trapshooting in the United States was at the Sportsmen's Club in Cincinnati in 1831. Live pigeons were used. In those days there was an abundance of game, and no doubt trapshooting and releasing game from traps gave the hunters practice. Domestic pigeons eventually replaced wild birds and wooden blocks, tin cans and bottles thrown in the air from behind a barricade.

Charlie Portlock of Boston introduced the first glass ball competition mentioned as trapshooting in 1866. Following that development many matches were staged on glass balls. The first glass ball champion was Capt. A. H. Bogardus.

These balls were the inanimate substitutes for pigeons and they attained wide popularity in the 1870s. However, none of the glass balls simulated the flight of a bird. The first really successful substitutes for balls was not found until George Ligowsky of Cincinnati invented the clay target. Remarkably enough, it closely resembled the clay targets of the present day.

Along with this new target, Ligowsky produced a practical ground trap for throwing it. The Ligowsky target and trap, first perfected in the early 1880s, gave trapshooting as we know it today its real start. The first National clay target championship was held in New Orleans in February, 1885.

That year Capt. Bogardus was hailed as the best shot in the land, but the indomitable "Doc" W. F. Carver won the championship. After that, in order, came J. A. R. Elliott, Rollo Heikes, Harvey McMurchy and Bill Crosby. These gunners held sway until Fred Gilbert came along from Iowa and entered the game.

In England, meanwhile, clay targets never quite caught on until live pigeons became illegal in 1924. Then England's best club, the West London Shooting Grounds, turned to the clays. During our visit there in 1952 we found this club using fifty clay bird traps in a "walkup" game very similar to our quail "walkups" now.

At the West London Shooting Grounds we shot with Harry Hensler, a famous big game hunter, and with Percy Stansbury, shooting instructor. Then, while in London, we took time to visit the big name gun makers—Churchill, Wesley Richards, Perdey, Boss, Cogswell and Harrison, Greener, Grant and Lang, John Rigby, W. J. Jeffrey, C. B. Vaughn, Holland and Holland and several others.

All of them own their own shooting grounds where they fit and test guns. My contacts with such illustrious names has rounded out my years of shooting as nothing else could have done.

Roger Preuss

CHAPTER FIVE

SIRENS of the FAR PLACES

Goose music, like sunsets, a beautiful woman, or fine brandy, can get in your blood. Once you've heard the eerie call wafted to you from afar on a high, chill wind, you are gone. Each year thereafter, when the autumnal equinox rolls around, a glassy film coats the eye and you find yourself staring into the distant horizon.

You have become a devotee of the wild, wild goose. You do not know how you got that way. All you recognize is that insistent gnawing at your vitals that all goose hunters know.

First, there is the call—the strident, insistent, provocative call of the wild goose. The faintest hint of the unforgettable sound has made men misty-eyed. Hunters have wakened in the night hearing the sound of geese, and they have been unable to go back to sleep. It's the call of the wild, the symbol of all the far places, the Siren Song of the North that beckons every goose hunter on to his wild chase of this elusive visitor from the sub-Arctic regions where no man trods.

I still remember the marrow-chilling effect of goose music over the prairies of southern Manitoba. I was only a boy, living and carrying my end of the work on a farm south of Morden. But even then the call of geese had a strange and electrifying effect on me.

Each spring the blues and snows would come north in countless echelons, wave after wave excitedly talking it up. They would congregate first at Whitewater lake by the tens of thousands. They would stay a few days to pluck at green shoots of small grains, then move on to Grants Lake a few miles from Winnipeg before making the final lap to their nesting grounds in the then unknown Arctic.

So there was spring shooting, and it was the spring of 1910 when I shot my first goose on Grandfather's farm south of Morden. Old Granddad Cruikshanks had a rare understanding of geese and guns and boys.

"Ya got to get a few black an' blue marks afore ya kin rightly say ya kin handle that ol' blunderbuss of mine," he told me. "Now git on out to them potholes an' get us a few mallards for supper."

The "Blunderbuss" was a rusty, well-worn, old 44-inch single barrel Zulu 12-bore shotgun, and it was all I could do to carry it, to say nothing of swinging it on a duck. But I had used it before, not only on ducks, but jackrabbits and prairie chickens. My mother had given me a hand loader for my birthday so I had a bag of hand-loaded shells.

The country around was alive with ducks, and the nearest pothole was a seething mass of mallards as I crawled on my belly to the brow of a hill and looked down into it. I snugged the old Zulu down onto an earth clod and prepared to pot me a mess of ducks. But a jagged rock cut into my ribs, so I rolled over to find a better spot. At that instant a terrific clamor of alarm went up immediately behind and above me.

Startled, I looked up at the frenzied confusion of the biggest flock of blue and snow geese I had ever seen. They were so near I could have hit one throwing my cap into the air.

It might have been instinct. Or the urgency of Granddad's order. I pointed the gun upward, closed my eyes and pulled the trigger. Then pain stabbed my thigh where my shoulder should have been. But amidst the excited babble of geese I heard the distinct thud of a heavy body. I opened my eyes. The geese were clawing air to gain distance off to my right. Dazed, I looked around and instantly forgot my pain.

I had shot a goose! It lay, an immense white mound, forty yards down the hill.

If I expected Granddad Cruikshanks to be elated when I got back home with the big snow dangling by the neck from my shoulder, I was doomed to be promptly deflated.

90

"Why, I believe the lad got hisself a goose," the old man said. "Thought I told ya to get a mess o' ducks fer supper."

A year or so later I thought I knew all there was to know about hunting geese. I had shot dozens of them. But I had that taken out of me when Bill Connor brought in a 22-pound Canada goose he had bagged at Whitewater Lake. It was the biggest goose I had ever seen before or since, and for many years it was on display at Morden. It may not be the biggest goose ever bagged, but show me a bigger one. Even 12-pound Canadas are rare. The average gander will weigh between nine and ten pounds, with the goose averaging seven to eight.

The greatest goose hunt I ever had was down the Saskatchewan River in northern Manitoba in September of 1939. We'd been shooting mallards and canvasbacks with Clark Gable at our duck club on the Delta Marsh at the south end of Lake Manitoba. On our way back through Portage La Prairie we met an old friend, Roxy Hamilton, owner of the Aberdeen Hotel in Winnipeg.

"You fellas are pikers," Roxy said. "Why don't you go with me on a real hunt—a goose hunt at The Pas? Horace Halcrow and I are leaving next week. I'll give you five minutes to make up your mind."

I didn't need the five. The following Monday I was back, with Telf Miller, Portage La Prairie hotel owner, in tow. Roxy and Barney Stitt of The Pas met us. With them were Halcrow, a dominion game conservation agent; Charlie Morgan, winner of world championship dog derbies at The Pas in 1919, 1920, and 1921; Joe Wong, a Chinese cook; and three Cree guides, Harold Wells, Charley Stevens and George McGilvrey. Tommy Lamb, noted bush pilot, was along to supervise the trip.

We boarded Lamb's gasoline-powered river boat, the "Skippy L.," and started down the Saskatchewan through mile after endless mile of low, flat bush country. At Hill Island we met George Dupre, game guardian, and he told us that twenty miles further down geese were as plentiful as ticks on a dog in spring. That night we camped with Jack Heard, another game warden, in his cabin near the spot Dupre had told us about.

Next morning Heard towed our canoes up a feeder stream and through several shallow lakes alive with geese. We flushed flock after flock, some of them swerving within twenty yards of us.

Clark Gable and guide Phil Ducharme trail back to the Sports Afield duck club after a great day in the marshes.

Photo by Jimmy Hamilton

We used Tommy Lamb's Skippy-L on our goose hunt on the Saskatchewan river, near The Pas, in 1939.

"If you're going to keep tempting me like this, I'll get a permanent cramp in my trigger finger," I told Heard.

"Keep your shirt on," he answered. "This is nothing. Wait'll we get in there."

That night we camped out and at sunup there was ice in the water bucket. I hadn't slept a wink, sharing one ground blanket with Roxy and Telf. We were up at 5:00, and the gray dawn was raw and sleety. Wong gave us a hearty breakfast of flapjacks, then we began breaking ice to get our canoes through a labyrinth of water leads in the muskeg. It had frozen quite hard during the night and a sharp nor'wester pelted our faces with sleet as Heard posted Roxy, Telf and myself on each side of a gravel bar at the head of a creek that drained two marshy lakes. Small patches of snow still remained here and there.

About seven o'clock a quartet of white-front geese (the Crees call them laughers) came swinging in between Miller and me. He took one of the left angle birds and I brought down two on the right with No. 6 loads. Then two more came in, easy shots, and we took care of them. More small flocks followed and soon we had ten geese down.

Now Tommy Lamb and the rest of the party moved in. By noon everyone had his limit of geese. As we pulled out for Heard's camp hundreds more geese continued to buck in for gravel in anticipation of their final take-off for the south. On the way back to our river boat we must have flushed twenty-five flocks of honkers, some sitting until we were within thirty yards of them before they got up.

Aboard the Skippy L. I was so exhausted from two sleepless nights I flopped on the floor of the cabin.

"Just cover me with a blanket and leave me be," I said. "Even if Roxy and Telf have nightmares tonight they won't keep me awake."

Every goose hunter I know will tell you geese are the smartest birds that fly, as smart as the wild turkey. But I have seen them do things as dumb as a redhead, like trying to get into your decoys while you're still setting them out. In any case, they occasionally do something completely off form, and one of the strangest stories I ever heard about geese concerned a big gander named Moses. Something like twenty years ago a flock of Canadas came north one spring day, crossed over the wildlife sanctuary near Portage La Prairie, Manitoba, and old Jim Ingels, manager of the sanctuary, saw one of the flock drop out. The others continued on north to the breeding place of their birth.

Jim figured the goose was either crippled, exhausted from the long flight, or a stranger in the flock. So he called him Moses and set out some feed for the big fellow. In due time Moses began taking a shine to one of Jim's crippled Canadas. Four young were eventually produced.

"That fall the same flock Moses had come north with appeared over the place," Jim told me. "They circled several times and called their heads off for Moses. So Moses got up and joined them and the last I saw they were all headed south."

But next spring Moses was back. The flock must have passed in the night, for Jim never saw them. He merely got up one morning and there was Moses, back to rejoin his mate who had wintered on the sanctuary. Jim enticed Moses into a cage so he could examine him for injuries and weigh him. The big gander tipped the scales at thirteen pounds.

"Well, Moses sired six more youngsters that spring," Jim said. "But he was off again with the flock when the first frosts came. The third year he returned again and produced four young ones."

Came the fourth spring and Moses was not among the flock that passed over the sanctuary. Either he had been killed or he had died of old age. His crippled mate stayed on two or three years more, then she, too, died of old age.

Even now old Jim Ingels, in his retirement, reflects upon the old gander with sadness and affection.

"That Moses, he was a fierce old boy. Once Jimmy Hamilton tried to get a closeup picture of him and he knocked the camera right out of his hands. But we loved him in spite of his temper."

Goose hunting usually doesn't develop too many laughs, because it's deadly serious business, but I once got a chuckle out of a hunt at Chamberlain, S. D., on the hilly banks of the Missouri River. Our host was Orie Derby, Chamberlain cafe owner and one of the state's top goose shots. With me were Harlow Curtice, now president of General Motors, and Harley Earle, automobile designer.

It was late in the season and the big flocks of honkers had moved down from Devils Lake in North Dakota and Sand Lake above Aber-

Canadas going out to feed.—Les Kouba

Gary Cooper duck hunting at Sun Valley with his black Labrador. Taylor Williams, head guide at Sun Valley, claims that Gary Cooper is the best big-game rifle shot he has ever hunted with.

Sun Valley Photo

deen to the warmer waters of the river. Each morning they would take off from the river, scramble for altitude to get over the broken hills, and move on out to feed in the picked cornfields back of the hills.

The night of our arrival in Chamberlain the thermometer did a nose dive, and by morning the temperature was 'a little below zero with a stiff northwest wind blowing. Snow covered the ground and more was slanting in on the wind as we climbed down into the pits Orie had dug in a cornfield.

I got into one pit with Curtice. Orie crowded his three hundred pounds into another with six-foot-four Earle. Both Orie and I began calling when we saw a big flock take off from the river and head up one of the draws. The geese responded perfectly.

As one string of the flock swung over our decoys, Curtice and I raised up. I cut loose with three shots. Two big honkers dropped out, hurtled downward and landed in the cornfield with that unmistakable thud of a dead goose. I turned to my pit companion.

"Well, Mr. Curtice, you have killed your first goose."

There was a look of amused tolerance on his face.

"Jimmy," he said, "you're just a plain liar. The safe on this over and under of mine was on. I didn't fire a shot."

Later, of course, we all filled out of Canadas, and ever since the Chamberlain area has always been one of my favorites for goose hunting.

Around Chamberlain they still talk about the wounded honker that flew into Donald Rosenberg's farm yard several years ago. The farm is on the banks of the Missouri, directly under the main goose flyway. So this gander made himself very much at home in the few days it took him to get acquainted with the Rosenberg tame geese and chickens. Rosenberg told me the story one day on a hunting trip with Tom Banks and Jack Clark.

"Had no trouble with hawks, owls or other predators after this honker had arrived," Rosenberg said. "Once this big gander even scared the wits out of a coyote that had his eye on some of my chickens."

When his injured wing had healed, and he was able to fly, he still elected to stay with his new found friends, even though flocks of wild geese were coaxing him daily to come along south. On the third year of his stay the big yard boss took unto himself a tame goose as a mate.

The last I heard from Rosenberg was that the union had been a fortunate one and several issues of progeny resulted.

No one can say with certainty how many geese of all the various species wing up and down the continent on their spring and fall migrations. But it's estimated more than a million blues and snows winter in Louisiana and along the Gulf coast of Texas. For massed concentrations of birds, no two states offer finer hunting possibilities. But southern methods of hunting geese are quite different from those in the north or on either coast.

I once hunted geese in Louisiana with Major Jim Brown, then game commissioner of the state. On the trip I made the acquaintance of the Louisiana "marsh buggy" for transportation and I learned about using sheets of newspaper for decoys.

The marsh buggy is a hybrid land-sea animal, half Ford, half tractor. It's capable of rolling over oozing mud and negotiating bulrushes in water four feet deep. Its principal advantage is that it gets you to your hunting spot and back, which you couldn't otherwise do without a helicopter. The newspaper decoys—well, we'll get to those. So I had my initiation in marsh buggy riding and hunting over newspapers, and I figured that was for me. No work getting there; no decoys to carry.

The next winter I brought Ted Culbertson of Minneapolis with me. He had hunted everywhere, and he knew all the answers. So why should I brief him on Louisiana methods? He could tell those Southerners a thing or two about goose hunting.

Now snows and blues on the Louisiana wintering grounds go out to feed shortly after sunup each morning. They return to the Gulf about nine o'clock. You make your spread on the mud among the bulrushes and bag your geese as they go to or from feed.

Sully Menard was piloting his marsh buggy the day Ted and I started out for the mud flats. The cottony sky was flecked with thousands upon thousands of geese going out to feed. Ted was restless as a mallard hen on a clutch of eggs. He had never seen so many geese in the air in all his life. Then his mouth slacked open as he saw the barren mud flat toward which Sully was heading.

"Hey, we forgot the decoys," he moaned. "How we goin' to get any geese in without decoys?"

I pulled a folded newspaper out of my hip pocket, and Pete, our Cajun guide, extracted one from his. "Here's our decoys—all ready to set up."

Sully dropped me off at the edge of one small mud mound and Pete began wrapping clods of mud in sheets of newspaper, one free end upward to resemble a goose's neck. When he had two dozen set out, Sully moved him and Ted to another nearby flat where the process was repeated.

Sully rejoined me and Pete called from Ted's blind, "Now watch 'em come in."

Come they did. Shortly before nine o'clock the huge flocks began coming back from their feed fields, headed toward the Gulf. As they spotted our newspaper decoys, perched on mud flats a foot deep, little groups would break off the main flocks and come gliding in. The calling of Sully and Pete encouraged them. In less than an hour we had our limit. It was one of the really great shoots I've had on snow and blue geese. For Ted it was a revelation. I thought, for a moment, we'd have to take away his shells to get him to stop shooting.

"I wouldn't have believed it if I hadn't seen it," he said. "Who prints that newspaper we used? First time I ever saw a newspaper that you could believe."

Another great goose shooting spot is on Chesapeake Bay, and to my way of thinking it may be just as good as Canada or Louisiana. Key Wallace, a federal warden, was in charge of the 10,000-acre goose refuge on the bay when I once went hunting on the nearby Robbins farm with Jack Seville, John Scott, the artist, and Ted Kesting.

We met Key after shooting our limit of canvasbacks on the bay, and he told us that the wintering flock of geese on his refuge had grown from 5,000 birds to 50,000 in a few years. To me it was an amazing thing, for the countryside around Chesapeake Bay is thickly populated. Most of the farmers in the area have to go no farther than the limits of their own property to bag geese.

Probably the continent's greatest hunting pressure, however, is on the geese concentrated at Cairo, Ill., in the "V" formed by the confluence of the Ohio and Mississippi rivers. Here, for countless genera-tions, Canada honkers have concentrated each fall.

Adjacent to the Horseshoe Lake refuge, but far enough away to provide a "buffer zone" prescribed by state law, are the gun clubs. Hunters from one end of the nation to the other come to these clubs each fall to bag their geese. When the Canadas rise from Horseshoe Lake to venture out for feed, the noise is like that of a thundering freight train.

As they gain altitude, constantly chattering to themselves, they fly over the hunting club pits just beyond the refuge boundaries. All along the line tense hunters rise up in their pits and guns bellow. Here and there, from the wavering strings of geese, a few fall to earth. The others veer away, swing back to the refuge and safety, or climb out to their feed.

That's the story of goose hunting at Cairo. For ten years I had been resisting the temptation to try the competition at Cairo. It didn't seem like a sporty proposition to me. But each year at the Grand American trapshoot I would be pressed by Bill Fienup, Hale Jones, and other Illinois shooters to give their "goose hunting capitol of North America" a whirl.

So, on an elk hunting trip to the Rockies one fall at the Covered Wagon Ranch with Benny Benson and Ray Ewald, my friend Earl Gerard of Minneapolis confessed to me he would rather bag one goose at Cairo than shoot all the elk in Montana. I figured Bill Fienup could satisfy Earl's craving so I wrote to him.

"Come down at once," was the answer.

Bill's gun club, owned by about twenty Illinois and Missouri shooters, was about thirty miles from Cairo on an island in the Mis-sissippi. Charlie Friar, his caretaker, rowed us over, and at 7 a.m. we were in the pits. Earl and Bill's son, Ray, were in the pit to the left, Bill and I in the center, Lew Barringer and Dr. Guy Rupe on the right flank. The weather was too good—70 in the shade with not a whiff of a breeze.

"Don't look like we're going to get any geese today," Bill said. "I'll just try a few blasts on this call anyway."

A string of honkers moving down the main river heard the call and veered over, but swung wide of our decoys. Bill was right. This was no day for goose hunting. So the next morning Earl, Hale Jones and I drove out to another club with Babe Yates, about twenty miles from Cairo. There must have been seventy anxious hunters waiting for the cars that would take us out to our blinds. We were dropped off at shooting pits along the road. A few minutes before the zero hour you could see heads popping up in all directions from the pits.

When the first flock appeared above the trees to our right the blasting started. The geese must have been three gun ranges high, but it didn't matter to these "Skybusters." Finally a flock came over the trees headed directly for us. We waited until we literally could see their eyes. Two dropped out. By eight o'clock we had seven geese and needed only two more for our limits. Those we dropped out of the next flock over us.

"You know," said Hale, "these guys we have down here are the greatest conservationists on earth. They just won't let the birds come in."

Some years ago Sports Afield assigned me to do a story on market hunting in Mexico. So I got Rusty Annabel, the Alaska writer, to go with me—a feat not too difficult, considering Rusty's weakness for adventure. At Guaymas we met Tommy Jamieson, who runs a fleet of fishing boats. He suggested we go out and shoot a few geese for diversion.

"I'm having a dinner for the mayor of Guaymas and I could use four or five geese anyway," he said.

We drove out to Obregon, south of Guaymas, in the heart of the goose country. I have never seen anything like it. The rice fields were literally jammed with thousands of white fronted geese, which in Canada we call "cacklers."

"But how are we going to get at them?" I asked Tommy. "We haven't any decoys, no pits, no blinds."

Tommy pointed to a tractor which one of the rice farmers had left standing in a field. "We'll borrow that tractor and you'll see how it's done in Mexico."

He started the machine and directed Annabel and me to hang on behind. Then he began circling a big flock of white-fronts in the nearest rice field. It was soon apparent they were used to tractors, for they paid not the slightest attention as Tommy kept narrowing the circle.

102

Then suddenly he headed the machine straight for the center of the geese. Alarmed by this strange antic, they clambered into the air.

Rusty and I jumped off the tractor and managed to get off three shots apiece. Five geese came tumbling down.

"That's the way we do it down here," said Tommy. "Now we've got enough meat for that dinner."

It was quite a bit short of my idea of sporty goose shooting. But it brought quick results. The next year, however, I took decoys to Mexico and found the birds as willing to cooperate on their wintering grounds as they are on the breeding grounds where they have to stoke up on food for the long journey south.

Every goose hunter I know takes the chase in dead seriousness, since the opportunities for shots come all too rarely. To some, the least infraction of the rules of the game is enough to blacklist the careless one. I have seen excellent shots never invited back because they dared to raise their heads to watch a flock of geese coming into a blind. But sometimes goose hunting has its moments of humor, too.

A few years ago I was hunting with the late Harry Fleischman of Los Angeles, Captain of my All-America team that year, and Alex Kerr, the Beverly Hills sporting goods dealer, one of the greatest skeet shots in this sport. Harry ran a gun club for Kerr and he operated a duck club for himself each year. Harry also played parts in western movies (he was a nephew of Max Fleischman of yeast fame) and many stars of the movie colony belonged to his club—Clark Gable, Carole Lombard, Robert Stack, Gary Cooper, Andy Devine, Robert Taylor, Bob Montgomery, Chet Laux and Tuffy Goff of Lum and Abner and other famous stars. So, as Alex Kerr and I were sitting in one of his blinds waiting for action, Harry regaled me with the story of the movie director who had a terrific shot on snow geese without even knowing it.

"This director came up to the club one day with a member and admitted he'd never shot a duck or a goose before," Harry said. "I put him out alone in the best blind we had and left him."

Meanwhile, Harry had a great day on geese himself, but at the end of the day the movie director came in completely dejected. He was disgusted with himself and all hunting. He had burned up two boxes of shells with not so much as a feather to show for it.

103

We lunched under canvas hunting geese on a cold, snowy day in northern Manitoba.

Photo by Chet Freden

Wings set, Canadas approach our blind.

Prince, our black Labrador, watches for ducks or geese as Doug Ewald and I push our Aluma craft through the mud.

"What's the matter?" Harry asked him. "From the sound of that blasting out there I thought you'd have birds for everybody in the club."

"Nah," the director said. "Nothing out there to shoot except sea gulls."

Harry walked out to the director's blind. When he got back he was toting nine snow geese he'd picked up around the blind.

"These your sea gulls?"

"Guess so," the director said.

"Mister, it's a good thing the game warden wasn't checking here today. You have just shot yourself over the limit of snow geese. Now I've got to give some to the farmers around here to keep us all legal."

California probably has as good goose shooting as you'll find anywhere in the country. One of the trips I'll always remember was on Len Browning's ranch near Grimes in northern California. Its roots go back to a duck hunt in Canada where my guests had been Baron Hilton, the hotel magnate, and Earl Stoner, one of the country's top skeet shooters.

By way of returning the favor, they invited me to go shooting with them on my next trip to California. During the afternoon at the Brown Derby, Hilton suddenly had a bright idea. "Let's fly up to Browning's and get ourselves a goose shoot."

Although I don't relish flying, Hilton was once a Navy pilot and if I could have confidence in anyone, I figured I should be able to trust Hilton with an airplane. As we circled Browning's ranch, I forgot my plane jitters when I saw thousands of blue snow geese on the chain of small lakes on his property.

This was different hunting. Browning had platform blinds built in the passes among the lakes, and his decoys were floaters. Small bunches of geese kept getting up to move out for feed, or merely out of restlessness. It was shooting deluxe, and getting a limit was no problem at all. But what amazed me was the deadliness of the little .410's the boys used.

"I never figured a .410 was any gun for geese," I told Baron, "but in your hands it sure brings them down."

Of course, all three are excellent skeet shots in all gauges, but more important, they let the geese come into close range before they pull the trigger, a virtue too many goose hunters forget. None of the three lost a single crippled goose that day.

106

On the whole, however, I would by no means recommend the .410 for the average goose hunter, even with three-inch loads. You need all the power and pattern you can get to bring down a 10-pound goose. The .12-gauge is the answer to that problem unless you are an expert like Hilton and Stoner and Browning.

After all these years of goose hunting, I'm sure that the quickest and easiest hunt I ever had was the last one I made late in the fall of 1955. I had just returned from my duck camp on the Delta Marsh and was sitting in my office catching up on paper work. The phone rang and I heard the familiar voice of Jack Dow, Minnesota chairman of Ducks Unlimited.

"Get yourself packed. You're going goose hunting in Wyoming with Bob Naegele, Tod Rauen and me. They say it's terrific out there, and I figure you must know someone who can take us out."

I thought of Adam Rexius, government trapper and rancher near Lusk, Wyoming. As a sideline, he makes some of the finest rubber goose decoys I've ever seen. So I got him on the phone and he confirmed the reports Dow had heard. That afternoon, we were aboard a plane bound for Casper, Wyoming, but before we had reached Rapid City, South Dakota, we were bucking into a blinding snowstorm and they grounded us at Rapid City.

There was nothing to do but hire a car to take us to Lusk. We made it the next morning over some of the worst hill roads I have ever traveled. A phone call from Lusk brought Rexius out on the double.

"Lots of geese in," he said. "Shouldn't have any trouble getting you into a good shoot."

He was more right than he knew. After changing to hunting clothes at the ranch, Rexius took us out to a seemingly endless expanse of barley stubble where he had dug his pits. We scarcely had time to get the decoys set out and make ourselves ready when the first flock from Canada headed straight in, without so much as a single call from us.

We dropped four out of that flock but before we could climb out of the pits to pick up the birds, Rexius shouted.

"Another big bunch heading in from the west. Get set!"

In they came, with all the confidence in the world. They were thirty yards high and their wings were set for a landing as they chattered their greetings to our lifelike decoys. Another volley of shots. Six more bodies tumbled to earth. We were all done.

"That," said Naegele, "was the quickest limit shoot on geese I've ever seen. It's a good thing the limit on honkers is two, a fellow could depopulate the country of geese around here."

One day Les Kouba, the famous wildlife artist who created the 1958 duck stamp, called me on the phone.

"Jimmy, I've got to see you before you take off for your duck camp in Manitoba."

I had just returned from the Grand American Trapshoot at Vandalia, Ohio, and was busy getting my Minneapolis office organized so I could take off the next morning for the Delta Marsh. Joe Walsh and Barry Bain had phoned that the mallards were eating Brian McCowan out of house and home. It was a clear case of having to go to the aid of a friend in need.

When Les showed up at the office, he had his old hunting pal with him, Vern Aanenson.

"Jimmy," he said, "I'll pay all your expenses if you'll take Vern and me on a goose hunting trip this fall. I've got to do some goose paintings and I want to go to the best place in the world to hunt geese."

It was a big order. How can you guarantee a goose will sit long enough for an artist to paint his picture? How can you guarantee you will get a goose shoot—anywhere? I've driven thousands of miles for geese—to some of the best shooting spots in America—and I've been skunked.

I thought of Remington Farms in Maryland where my friend Henry Davis holds forth. I'd hunted there the year before with Ted Kesting, Jack Seville, and artist John Scott from our New York office, and I remembered the geese were so thick they all but crawled down the gun barrel.

I could have contacted Red Dutton, the once famous hockey player and former manager of the New York Americans. He was now in Calgary and owned upwards of a jillion acres of fine goose country in northern Alberta. Or I could have grabbed the phone and called Don Conklin at Estes, Saskatchewan, or Tommy Lamb of The Pas in Manitoba. Tommy had offered to fly me into York Factory on Hudson's Bay for geese.

Sam Nickerson snaps Ki Steiner in front of our tent on a Canadian goose hunt, near Moose lake, in Manitoba.

Photo by Sam Nickerson

Vern Aanenson bags a pair of Canadas at Babe Yates goose camp near Cairo, Illinois.

Photo by Art Smith, Sleepy Eye

Then there were Ernest Jelley and Ralph Kohler, both famous trapshooters down in Missouri and Nebraska. They had exhausted their resources trying to get me to come down so they could teach me something about goose shooting.

I showed Les a few of the letters on my desk. One was from Art Storz, the Omaha brewer, who owns one of the finest goose clubs in America on the Platte River. Virg Mylan and I had hunted with Art a few years back. The other letter was from Ernie Paynter, Saskatchewan Game Director.

"Come on up and have a goose hunt with us this fall," Ernie's letter said. "Herb Moulding and Tom Sterling have spotted a terrific place." And one from Jim McMaster who has hunted over fifty consecutive years at Westbourne, Manitoba. "Bud Scharien and Slim Skaftfeld were wondering if you could spare a couple of days and hunt with us this fall? Slim (a blacksmith) has made a flock of tin decoys that should pull them in."

There were a hundred and one places I could have taken Les and Vern. But to guarantee them geese — that was something else. Then the answer came to me.

"We will go to Cairo, Illinois," I said. "We'll hunt with Babe Yates who runs a camp near the Horseshoe reserve."

Babe, I knew, had hunted geese since he was knee high to a shotgun hull. The geese around Cairo were so well acquainted with him he could feed them out of his hand.

When I got back from relieving Farmer McCowan's mallard problems at Delta Marsh, Les, Vern, and I took off for Illinois, joined by Grove Forester of Minneapolis and Art Smith of Sleepy Eye, Minnesota. Babe and an Illinois Conservation Department Public Relations man named Jim Helfrich, met us at Cairo.

"Jim will show you the Horseshoe refuge first so you can get your pictures," Babe explained. "Then I'll take you over to my camp and show you greenhorns the rudiments of shooting geese."

They say the Yates brothers are the greatest goose hunters in the world, and I don't doubt it. The seven brothers have lived all their lives on the Mississippi River, and they've hunted it since they were old enough to get a gun up to their shoulder.

Babe has shot so many geese he actually looks like one. His six-foot-five frame is so lanky it resembles nothing so much as a goose's neck. Then there is Spike, who runs the Lakeside Hunting Club, largest at Cairo with thirty-three pits; and there is "Too-Tall," who takes in hunters at his Hoosier Camp. Not to mention Johnny, the oldest, Foster and Chesley, all over six feet. The seventh was Asa, killed some years ago while hunting.

We made our headquarters at the Goose Pit where hunters foregather every evening to boast about stone-dead kills. Babe told us there were more than 200,000 geese in the Cairo area, gathered on four refuges. Horseshoe was the largest with 105,000 birds. Then there were the Union, Crab Orchard and the smallest Mermat refuges.

The clubs charged only $10 a day, with two geese per day allowed and you could shoot from sunrise to 3 p.m. Here, more than 30,000 hunters concentrate each fall at the seventy-five commercial and private clubs. Their take runs around 22,000 geese. Adding twenty-five per cent for cripples, it was evident the total goose population at Cairo is not threatened by hunting. Officials can shorten or lengthen the season at will to adjust the take to the harvestable population, and as soon as the prescribed number of geese are harvested, the hunting is shut off.

Illinois has a public shooting grounds for residents only in the area and the charge is only $2 a day. But the limit is one goose per hunter and shooting stops at noon. The public shooting grounds can handle a hundred hunters a day who draw for pits two hundred yards apart. All in all the refuge and shooting areas are operated very successfully, both from the standpoint of sustained yield for hunters and for preservation of the goose flocks.

Our first day in the refuge for pictures was a revelation, not only to Les and Vern, but to myself, although I had seen geese by the thousands in many parts of the land. It was a raw, windy day with leaden skies, the kind of provocative weather that kept geese moving all day.

We sat simply amazed at the spectacle. The birds came off the refuge not by the thousands, but by the tens of thousands. There was never a moment of the day when you could not look up and see the sky full of geese. Les shot pictures and made sketches until he was dizzy from swiveling his head.

Our goose hide at Cairo.

Les Kouba, who painted the 1958-'59 migratory duck stamp.

Next day we went out in the morning to hunt and Grove Forester got his limit within a few minutes. Then he left to return to Minneapolis, leaving Vern and Art to do most of the shooting.

On the third day, his camera work and sketching done, Les wanted to try his hand. We were in a woods pit called Possum Patch that morning and Jim Helfrich had told us some newly arriving flocks had built up goose population to its peak for the season. Now I could agree. The day was cold, wet and miserable; the birds were milling about in indescribable numbers. We sat there enthralled by the unbelievable spectacle.

I had seen northern duck flights take off from the Delta Marsh in Manitoba when the air seemed to be so full of ducks you couldn't pack another one in the sky. That was on Cadham Bay with Burr Tarrant and George Briggs from Eau Claire, Wisconsin, last November. Burr and George had never seen more ducks, and I had to admit that neither had I.

But now we were seeing geese in similar sky-packed flocks. They just kept coming and coming, flock after flock, until the horizon on all sides was filled with geese. In a lifetime of hunting geese I had never seen anything like it. I sat there without firing my gun, but it was worth the price of my train ticket to Cairo just to be there on this unforgettable day.

Les was similarly impressed. "No artist could paint this picture," he said. "No one would believe it if he did. This is just indescribable."

Art and Vern, meanwhile, had been firing away in the next blind. It didn't take them long to fill out, then they, too, sat and just looked. Art took movies until he ran out of film, then, finally, the two of them walked over to our blind.

"My life is complete now," said Vern. "I've seen all the geese in the world."

CHAPTER SIX

GHOST MOOSE and a PHANTOM MUSKIE

Some people can get all lathered up at the mere mention of the word "moose." For them a trip into the back country to hunt the so-called lord of the forest is like getting a passport to heaven. I killed my first moose up in Manitoba way back in 1920, and I must say I wasn't too impressed. It was too easy.

My second moose, some years later, did nothing to elevate the species as one that could provide the thrill of a lifetime. With me on that trip was Walter Wilwerding, the now famous wildlife painter. The year was 1931 and we had moved far back into Bleak Bay on Rainy Lake to get some local color for a series of moose sketches Wilwerding was doing.

Unfortunately, the big bull I shot was dropped three miles back in heavy timber. Even before we could dress the animal out it started snowing. By the time we lugged the quarters back to camp we were ploughing knee deep through the white stuff. To this day I haven't fully recovered from that ordeal. It left me with an avid distaste for moose hunting.

Over the years I have always been, by preference, a duck and goose man. That doesn't involve so much hard labor and, to my way of thinking, it's a much sportier shooting proposition.

But there was one day on Lake Anishinabi in northern Ontario that brought me back into the fold of the moose hunting clan.

Purple afternoon shadows were stretching out from the spruce-lined shore and the lake was as silent as an empty church. Joe Loon, our Indian guide, broke the spell.

"Moose over there. Big bull. In the lily pads."

I stared in the direction of the lifted arm. Then I laid my fishing rod across the gunwales. Joe dipped his paddle and moved us with the stealth of a cat toward the dark shape ahead. Not once did water drip from the paddle as he sculled us forward. At thirty yards he stopped the canoe. The bull turned and surveyed me with calm eyes. He was belly deep in the pads and reluctant to leave the succulent stems.

"You ever shoot moose?" Joe whispered.

I admitted I had, but was not too impressed. However, this rack was spectacular. It would, indeed, be a trophy. But the whisper was enough. The moose swiveled his ponderous antlers, clamored out of the pads and disappeared into the spruce.

"You come up this fall," Joe said. "I take you to moose bigger than this."

"How can anything be bigger than that?" I asked.

"Below Manitou Falls on English River I show you ghost moose of Barker Lake. He is bigger."

It was an unbelievable tale. A tale of a mammoth moose that had eluded hunters for years. "Now you see him, now you don't," Joe explained. "Ghost moose. Lots of hunters try for him but nobody can get close enough."

So I was hooked, as I have said. We started back for our rendezvous with Barney Lamm's airplane. Joe never liked to guide fishermen anyway, and we had had enough of Lake Anishinabi's six-pound lake trout. I knew he much preferred hunting and was waiting only for the moose season to open.

"You come October first," said Joe. "We go for ghost moose. Shoot ducks, too. And I show you muskies. Biggest muskies you ever saw below the falls."

Barney was waiting for us in his plane when we got to the rendezvous. If more bait were needed to get me out moose hunting, Barney

116

provided it when we arrived at his main camp on Ball Lake, forty-five miles north of Kenora, Ontario. He confirmed everything Joe had told me, not only about the ghost moose, but about ducks and a giant musky that had eluded his best efforts over several seasons.

"That musky will weigh sixty pounds if it goes an ounce," Barney added. A flyer in World War II, he was a quiet, soft-spoken and completely honest man. I had never caught him in an exaggeration.

"I'd like to see you get a crack at this ghost moose," he continued. "They tell me you were a dead shot sniper with the Canadians in the first World War. But I doubt even you could bag him."

Joe chimed in. "Me, too. Jimmy too fat. He smoke too many big, black cigars. He talk too much in boat to get moose."

Back in Minneapolis the challenge of the ghost moose and 60-pound muskies plagued me for weeks. When I related the story to Jack Connor, outdoor editor of the Minneapolis Star-Tribune, he nearly flipped his lid.

"Deal me in," Jack said. "I can't miss that trip. What a story!"

A little later I bumped into George Hart and a light flashed on. Here was our ideal third man. We'd need a truck to get that moose back home, and George was in the trucking business. Besides, he'd been a lifelong hunting companion. Would he like to go?

"Would I?" George grabbed quick. "When do we leave? I'll probably have to shoot that moose for you, though."

It was the last week in September when we pulled away from Minneapolis. George's truck was loaded with sleeping bags, an assortment of rifles and shotguns, fishing tackle and cameras. We checked through the border at Fort Francis, Ontario, with no more trouble than signing our names to gun and travel permits. At dusk we were in Kenora where Pete Hughes had reserved hotel accommodations. His Kenora agent, Charlie Stevens, was waiting in the office for us.

"Barney just called by short wave from Ball Lake," Charlie said. "He'll pick up the three of you here tomorrow in the twin engine Cessna."

We marveled at the convenience of Barney's short wave intercom between his Kenora office and the Ball Lake camp forty-five miles away. At any time of the day or night Barney could get in instant touch with Kenora. Should an emergency require a doctor he could be summoned and flown to the camp within half an hour. Two-way radio communication has become a necessity of camp operation in northern Ontario's airplane country.

Tired by the long drive from Minneapolis, we hit the sack early. But halfway through the night George was awakened by a scuffling noise in the hotel room the three of us occupied. He sat bolt upright, then nudged Jack awake.

"Where's that confounded light switch?" George asked. Jack fumbled for the head lamp and switched it on.

"Well, I'll be . . ." He faltered for words. "Robinson is up to his old sleep-walking tricks. Shades of World War I. Hey! What the devil do you think you're doing, Jimmy?"

Apparently I was crawling along the floor on my hands and knees. I came awake slowly and rubbed my eyes. "No, it wasn't the enemy. I thought I was creeping up on that ghost moose."

Promptly at nine the next morning Barney glided up to the Kenora city dock in the Cessna. We stowed away duffel, guns and other gear while the plane was being gassed.

"I've already flown up to Manitou falls with a couple of canoes and three guides, including Joe Loon," said Barney. "They're setting up the moose camp for you now."

The plane roared away, circled Kenora once to gain altitude, then headed for Ball Lake. Below a beautiful panorama of rock outcroppings, spruce forest and sparkling lakes unfolded. George got out his movie camera and took half a reel of scenery. Within thirty minutes we were making the long glide earthward for a landing at the Ball Lake camp.

On the way up to camp headquarters we passed Barney's walk-in freezer building. "Got something to show you in there," he said. "Come on in." He lifted up a huge musky.

"Wow!" George was impressed. "How much did that one weigh?"

"Just forty-five pounds. Ki Steiner caught it the other day right in front of this camp. But he lost it trying to land the fish. Next day my wife Marian found it washed up on shore. It's still fifteen pounds short of the one you fellows are going after at Manitou Falls."

We walked up the graveled path toward headquarters. George,

dedicated to his "pitcher" taking, as he called it, was concentrating on Marian's pet fawn. At the moment it was nudging her hand for sweets. Then a moose calf stepped into the scene. George abandoned the fawn forthwith and swung on the moose calf.

It had been picked up as a helpless, orphaned baby by one of the Indian guides on Lake Anishinabi several months before. Brought back to Ball Lake, it nursed a bottle for weeks but seemed to gain little weight. Then Barney tried out a baby food mash and the calf approved heartily. It was still in the gawky, awkward stage but had been gaining weight rapidly.

We got away the next morning with the plane more heavily laden than ever. Now, in addition to all our gear, it carried groceries to last us for a week. As we bore north the country below grew wilder each mile. We peered down at the maze of lakes and streams, hoping for a glimpse of a moose. Barney was following the winding course of the English River, and before we knew what it was, the white foam of a spectacular waterfall caught our eye.

"That's it," Barney shouted above the roar of the engine. "Manitou Falls. Those patches of white on the river bank below the falls are the tents your Indians have set up."

He circled once, then put the plane in a steep angle of descent and we skimmed down over the falls through an aisle of spruce that seemed to reach out to touch the wings. None too sure of myself at best in an airplane, I held my breath in fear that we'd crash any moment.

From the river bank the falls were even more impressive than they had seemed from the air. Huge, trembling masses of white water cascaded down over jagged rocks to end in a foamy series of eddies below. It looked like perfect fishing water. The pool below the falls was a quarter mile wide.

Here was a temptation too great for Jack. Before our three guides had unloaded our duffel, he broke out a casting rod and tossed a spoon into the eddies. The first cast produced a four-pound walleye; the next, its twin. In ten minutes he laid out enough walleyes for our noon dinner.

Meanwhile, George had disappeared into the birch and alders back of the tents. While he was gone Barney roared away for Ball Lake with the parting words, "I'll be back day after tomorrow to haul out your moose." When the last echoes of the plane's motor had died away, the droning music of the falls was punctuated by four shots.

Not long after George puffed into camp toting a brace of partridge. Joe Loon and Bob Rheault, French woodsman and World War II veteran, began steaking out Jack's fish. John Kelly, Indian trapper, cleaned George's birds.

"Think I'll try for that musky in the morning," Jack said as he gazed speculatively into the campfire that night. "You sure you know where he is, Joe?"

"Yeah," the Indian grunted. "Johnny, he take you down where he lies near the rushes below camp."

After breakfast next morning I got out a deck of cards and invited George to participate in a friendly little game. But George would have none of it.

"I've been a sucker for you long enough," he said. "Why don't you teach Joe the game?"

An Indian playing gin rummy? Now there was an idea. I called Joe over. "You like to play gin rummy, Joe?"

Jack had already departed camp and was heading downstream for the rushes with Johnny paddling. I got the story from him later. Just outside the rushes Jack snapped on a big tear-drop spoon and cast into a pocket. A big tail swirled water and Jack had a fish. But it was a northern which Johnny estimated at fifteen pounds. They tossed it back. Muskies were their game, not "jackfish," as the Canadians call the northern.

Several more casts to the edge of the rushes as they drifted along silently produced nothing. Then Jack cast to another pocket, but the spoon snubbed up tight and he couldn't get it back.

"Hold it, Johnny!" he said. "I'm snagged. Back us up to that pocket."

Several jerks of the rod failed to free the bait. Whipping the line was equally futile. Then it happened. There was an explosion in the water and a tremendous fish leaped clear.

"My God!" Jack turned pale as fog on a marsh.

"That's him!" Even Johnny was excited. "You got the big 'un on."

120

"Careful, now! Careful, Johnny! Pull out into the stream. Get us away from those rushes."

The guide edged the canoe away from the bulrushes, but the musky had ideas of his own. As he felt the pressure he started downstream. After thirty or forty feet he stopped.

Once again Jack put pressure on the line. This time the big fish made a washtub-sized boil in the water. He made three more runs. Half an hour later, almost as beaten as the fish, Jack brought his musky alongside.

"Pull for shore!" he snapped. "Gotta beach this baby."

Johnny swung the canoe around the tail end of the rushes and headed for a mud flat where the monster could be beached. The musky came along docilely enough now. To Jack he looked at least five feet long. Surely this must be the 60-pounder Barney had mentioned.

As the prow touched bottom Johnny leaped out and, sinking to his knees in the mud, he began pulling the canoe up to the bank. Jack stepped out of the bow onto solid ground and began to hand-line the fish in. It happened at that moment.

When the leviathan felt his belly grate against the bottom he decided he wanted none of it. With one powerful stroke of his paddle-wide tail, he lunged outward.

Snap! The 30-pound line parted.

In a flash the musky was gone. Then, a moment later, he leaped clear of the water, stood on his tail shaking his head and the Paul Bunyan spoon went flying out into the deep.

"Oh, no!" Jack sat down on the bank and buried his head in his arms.

"Too bad." Johnny was sympathetic. "But it was the same before with the others. Now you see 'im, now you don't."

"Yeah, he's gone, all right," sighed Jack. "Gone like a phantom. My phantom musky. Well, more power to him."

It was a silent trip back to camp. Lost in his morose thoughts, Jack was brought up sharply by the crack of four shots back in the bush.

"They can't be shooting rabbits again," he said. "That sounded more like a rifle. Now what are they after?"

He found me snoozing in the main tent. Joe and George were gone. Bob was casting for walleyes from the rocks. "They went out for deer," he explained.

An hour later George and Joe appeared, dragging a big buck behind them.

"He was standing at the edge of a swamp not over a quarter of a mile from here," George said. "Now we got camp meat. How'd you make out with the musky?"

"Blew it," Jack offered. "Tried to beach him and he snapped the line."

"So-oo-o," George taunted. "I had to get a deer for you. Now it looks like I'll have to catch that musky for you, too."

Jack's bellow of indignation aroused me from my slumber. After I'd been briefed on his phantom musky and George's successful deer hunt, it seemed like the next logical step was to try for some mallards.

"Why not?" Jack was enthusiastic now. "The moose season doesn't open until tomorrow."

Jack, Joe and I climbed into one canoe, George, Johnny and Bob into the other, and we started downstream past the scene of the disastrous encounter with the musky. Soon the river opened into beautiful Barker Lake. With Jack on the bow paddle, Joe in the stern angled the canoe toward the right and headed for a marsh half a mile away. The other canoe followed in our wake.

By now the afternoon sun was slanting toward the jagged line of spruce on the shore of the lake. Ahead I could see a pocket of open water in a vast expanse of bulrushes, and suddenly there was an outbreak of squawking as a dozen big mallards climbed almost vertically out of the pocket. We were too far for a shot, but it was all I needed just to see those ducks get up.

"All right, we'll put the two canoes into the rushes, one on each side of that pocket," I said. "Must have been good feed in there, or they wouldn't have been there. So they'll be back."

We hadn't long to wait. "Ducks coming from south," Joe Loon pointed to a distant flock. I got out the horn and blew a come-in call. The birds veered and headed for the pocket.

"Don't anybody shoot 'till I signal," I warned.

122

"Yeah." George was grinning. "He always says that. But before you can fire he's got two ducks down. Me, I'm taking them when they're in range, signal or not."

There were eleven fat mallards in the flock, and judging by the barrage we sent up not one of them should have escaped. As it was we picked up eight. This without so much as a single decoy. But, as I had predicted, the pocket was loaded with food.

In the next half hour they came in by singles, threes and fives. When we had sixteen down it was time to call a halt to shooting. We had all we could eat in two days. So we sat on and just watched the lovely sight of mallards pitching down to feed.

In camp that evening the discussion turned to strategy for the campaign against the ghost moose. He was given to hanging out near the mouth of a sluggish stream which drained a big swamp far back in the spruce. It flowed into Barker Lake at a marsh not far from where we had been shooting ducks. Joe and Bob had scouted the spot before our arrival. They had seen fresh tracks of a giant bull leading down a game trail to the marsh.

"He's around, all right," Joe commented. "We paddle up there later tonight and try to call him just for fun."

George, Joe and I took the first canoe, Jack, Bob and Johnny the second. Silently, nerves tense in expectation, we entered the mouth of the moose creek. The temperature was just at the freezing point and eddies of mist rose from the water-like wraiths. No wonder they called this the ghost moose.

We halted behind a screen of rushes. There was no wind at all. Joe cupped his hands and gave out with a low, gutteral grunt, not unlike the honk of a Canada goose. Then another, and another.

Silence. We scarcely dared breathe.

Then, out of the night-drenched shore willows, came an answering grunt. Joe waited. There was no more sound. He called once more. Again the answer, this time a little nearer. Now we could hear splashing as the moose entered the water. Every eye strained for a glimpse of a massive head rising up above the rushes.

What a moment for my asthma to take over. I tried with super-human effort to choke back a cough. It wouldn't be choked. As the raucous sound rent the still night we heard a mighty splash, then something crashing through the spruce, then silence again.

Resort owner Barney Lamm, hunter, fisherman, pilot and host.

Jimmy and Jack Connor.

Guide Joe Loon watches guide Bob Rheault and Johnny Kelley fry wall-eyes for dinner.

"Ghost moose." Joe was calmer than I. "Now he here. Now he gone."

But at least we had glimpsed our prize. It was encouraging to know that he had not fled the country. And tomorrow was another day. We paddled back to camp in high spirits.

Long before dawn Johnny and Bob had breakfast ready—flapjacks and bacon. The river was lost in an eerie fog and the black pre-dawn was so still it seemed actually oppressive.

This was the plan: Jack, Bob and Johnny would post themselves at the game trail running down to the marsh. George, Joe and I would paddle into the stream mouth again and try to call the moose out.

"No cough, now!" Joe warned. "This time it's for keeps."

How Joe found the stream in the fog and darkness I'll never know. Perhaps he had the instincts of a moose. The first gray light of dawn added a peculiar luminosity to the fog. But we could see nothing. It was like flying in a cloud. The world was lost in a gray-white shroud.

We waited at the stream mouth, hoping the first rays of the sun would lift the fog. Gradually a pink-tinted glow crept into the whiteness all around the fog blanket lifted perceptibly.

Joe sent out his challenge to the bull. Then he froze into attentiveness. Uttering no sound, he pointed out across the marsh to a dark mass rising out of the rushes just beneath the lifting floor of the fog.

It was the ghost moose!

He was standing belly deep in water. Only his back and huge antlered head showed above the rushes. It was a perfect broadside shot at 300 yards.

No muffing this one, I thought. Slowly I raised my .300 Weatherbee and peered through the Bausch and Lomb scope. I put the cross hairs on the bulk of the shoulder, took a deep breath, exhaled part of it and held. The cross hairs steadied. I began to squeeze off the trigger.

The first shot fractured the stillness of the morning. The moose didn't budge.

"High," Joe whispered.

I steadied the heavy barrel and brought the cross hairs down on the shoulder. Then I squeezed off.

At the shot the big moose dropped like a critter hit over the head in a slaughter house.

126

"Got 'im!" George blurted.

Seizing a paddle, he helped Joe push the canoe toward the moose, fighting both the rushes and underwater vegetation. The moose lay on his side in three feet of water fifty yards from solid ground.

"It's him!" Joe was exultant. "Ghost moose. Be careful. Maybe he not dead. Better shoot again."

George complied by putting his own 30.06 slug through the massive neck of the animal.

Half an hour later we were still trying to figure out how to drag the moose to dry land when Jack and the two guides paddled up. It required all six of us to get the big hulk in. Puffing from the effort, we stood around admiring the huge rack of antlers. They bore the marks of battle in several broken prongs.

"He'll go 1,500 pounds," Johnny estimated. "Maybe more."

Joe began the task of removing the cape and head of the moose while Bob severed the four quarters. We loaded all this into one canoe and Joe started back to camp alone with the burden. He promised to return for George and me later.

Barney arrived on schedule with the plane later in the afternoon. We managed to get the four quarters of the moose in the cabin, but the head and cape were too big to be squeezed through the door. So Barney strapped it on one pontoon.

Then George, Jack and I climbed in with all the moose meat and several glances of apprehension were directed at the head roped onto the pontoon. But, after a long run down the river and out into Barker Lake, Barney got the ship airborne.

Circling over Manitou Falls, we looked down to catch our last glimpse of our beautiful campsite. None of us ever would forget the moments of pleasure and the thrills we'd had there. Forty-five minutes later we were back at the Ball Lake camp.

"What a trip!" George exclaimed as we stepped off the plane. "We finally got the ghost moose. It'll probably be the best trophy to come out of Ontario this year."

"Right," Jack agreed. "And I'll have the best trophy next year when I come back for that phantom musky."

"You will at that," George agreed, "if I catch him for you."

"intails at Dawn" from an oil sketch by Roger P

my FIRST and LAST MARKET HUNT

Old Grandpa Cruikshank was as full of ideas as a worm-stuffed robin when it came to hunting. Right now the old Civil War veteran was proud as a peacock for wiping my eye more than once on a pair of flaring mallards. I honestly believe he would have turned around and headed right back for the grain fields we'd just hunted in Montana and Saskatchewan if I had merely hinted I'd like to get even.

But we were homeward bound for Winnipeg with all the ducks we could use . . . and there was a little matter of me getting a job.

"Well, what next?" Grandpa cocked a quizzical eye in my direction.

"Oh, I don't know. Think I'll get a job with some threshing rig. Ought to put me in shape for hockey this winter."

"Now thet's a gol-durned foolish thing t' do." The old man grunted his disapproval. "'Specially when th' duck season's jest gettin' started."

Grandpa always aimed for a weak spot. After four years with the 44th Canadian Infantry Battalion in France during World War I, I was long overdue for a bellyfull of duck hunting. I used to dream of it huddled in soggy trenches all over the front. Then I came home to play baseball all summer and Grandpa Cruikshank never missed a game. As a reward, when the baseball season ended, he took me on this hunt to Montana and Saskatchewan.

I'd come off a poor second, being more adept with rifles and grenades than scatterguns. It made the old man happy, but it stirred memories for me . . . memories of my pre-war youth on duck sloughs in Minnesota and Manitoba. Somehow, getting a job didn't seem so important after all.

Grandpa Cruikshank was mumbling, "If ya must get a job, I gotta friend named Bean from Minneapolis that owns a big ranch back in Saskatchewan. Near Bredenbury. He'll be needin' some hands for th' harvest. Hear tell th' ducks are eatin' up his crop, too."

Within a week the west-bound passenger train had me aboard, headed for Bredenbury along with a couple dozen other harvest hands. In my bag were two shirts, socks, an army blanket, a deck of cards, shoes and a pair of overalls—all I owned in the world.

There was no one to meet us at Bredenbury and no station agent. So we slept on the station floor, glad enough for a roof over our heads, and I was dreaming of skies darkened by millions of ducks when I was jolted awake.

"Goin' t'sleep all day, boy?" A white-haired man was standing over me, nudging me with his foot . . . Bean's timekeeper. "Five a.m. an' we got thutty miles t'go."

Ten minutes later we were bumping across country in a battered old Ford hung together only by the grace of God and some bailing wire. If there were any roads in the country, I didn't see them. We made it to the headquarters camp in time for a hearty breakfast, and then I met the ranch foreman, a mountainous ex-farmer from Kansas named MacKenzie. When we had finished eating he wasted no time getting down to cases.

"We got thirty sections of grain t'get in before th' snow flies," MacKenzie grumbled. "Got three steam threshin' rigs a-goin'. So there'll be no loafin'. But ya can pick yer job. Drivin' team pays $6 a day. Same fer field men. Spike pitchin' $7."

"I'll take spike pitchin'," I spoke up. "I can use that extra dollar."

The old timekeeper came up with the rickety Ford and hauled us five miles south to one of the bunk houses where we changed to overalls. Before noon I was pitching bundles to the hungry maw of a

130

threshing machine. I was soon wondering if I hadn't picked the wrong job.

I'd helped on Grandpa's threshing outfit before the war, but then a boy could knock off and go duck hunting when he got tuckered. There were no rest periods in the Bean operations. Three machines whirled from dawn to dark, each grinding out six or seven thousand bushels of oats a day. Ducks were feeding everywhere on the stubble left by the binders, but the machines kept me so busy pitching bundles I had few idle moments to steal a glance at ducks.

And then the rains came.

For two days we sat around the bunkhouse playing poker. A big Swede named Ole Larson, who had started with the harvest down in Kansas, was winning all our money. He couldn't lose. It was beginning to tell on the morale of the camp, and the enforced idleness didn't help any. Tempers flared at the slightest provocation, my own included, for now ducks were pouring in from the north and jamming every field.

One night, after the Swede had made a big killing, a hand called me outside the bunkhouse. "Robinson, did you notice anything wrong with the game tonight?"

"If I had, I'd have kicked like a steer," I said. Then I remembered that Ole always took the cards back to his own bunk after the game. He was already asleep and snoring, so the hand and I went through his bag. We found two decks and took them out under the light of a kerosene lamp. There were red ink spots on the backs of all the aces and face cards. No wonder Ole's luck held up. He knew nearly every card we had.

We woke up all the losers and showed them the marked cards. Ole was routed out at once and kangaroo court was convened on the spot. Ole never had a chance. Two of the threshers held his arms while another searched his pockets and bunk. Out came all the money he'd won . . . more than two thousand dollars. We got our money back and Ole acquired two of the most beautiful shiners I had ever seen.

But the incident left the whole camp in a surly mood, and it didn't improve the next day when we awoke to find a leaden sky still drenching the sodden land with a steady downpour. Some of the hands checked out and big MacKenzie was getting plenty worried.

Then I had an idea. The country was full of sloughs and we could see ducks milling everywhere, trading from water holes to the sagging grain. I hitched a ride to the headquarters camp that noon and broached MacKenzie.

"The boys are gettin' kinda restless," I told him. "Maybe a good duck dinner would set 'em up better. In this kind of weather I might as well be hunting. So if you got a gun around here I'll go out and knock off a duck dinner for everybody."

MacKenzie's tense face relaxed a shade. "Say, boy, thet might be th' ticket. I got an old two-pipe hammer gun here. Have th' timekeeper get ya some shells and go to it."

Back at the bunkhouse one of the bundle pitchers, a kid from Milwaukee, saw me getting ready. He suggested that if I didn't mind he'd tag along. He was getting to feel a bit creepy himself.

There was one big slough three miles from the bunkhouse that must have contained half the ducks in the world. By four o'clock that evening the bundle pitcher and myself were wading through it jumping pintails and cans in all directions. The big, white-bellied canvasbacks looked as large as geese. A cold snap further north had brought them down by the thousands, and the flight was on. When my shots folded them they hit the water like blazing, white meteors.

We brought back twenty ducks and I gave them to the cook. There was no grumbling among the hands after supper that night.

During the night a sharp temperature drop froze ice on all the sloughs. Next morning, although it had stopped raining, the grain was still too wet to thresh. So Milwaukee Barney and I lit out again for the big slough with a sharp northwest wind whipping our faces. About a mile from the bunk house we jumped a flock of prairie chickens.

"What kind of birds are those?" Barney asked.

"Yellow legs . . . prairie chickens," I answered. "Mighty good eatin', too."

There must have been fifty birds in the flock. Chickens start bunching in Saskatchewan at this time of the year . . . October. This flock was so tame we could walk right up to the birds, and I remember thinking they probably had never heard a shotgun report before.

I bagged a dozen from the flock before they were well scattered. Barney stowed them in a gunny sack he was carrying. Then we moved on toward the big slough. Biting eddies of sleet were now slanting down through the wind and ahead we could see ducks milling in preparation for heading south. The shooting was the kind you dream about. We had two dozen ducks in less than half an hour, but the weather was getting rougher by the minute.

"Think we'd better head for the bunkhouse," I told Barney. "Looks like this could turn into a real blow."

By the time we arrived at the cook shack it was snowing so hard we could barely make out the dark lines of the building. The cook had stew ready and we were just sitting down to it when the straw boss poked his head into the shack.

"MacKenzie wants to see you after supper," he said.

An hour later I was sitting in Boss MacKenzie's big front room at the main camp. He was puffing a fat cigar.

"Those ducks the cook served last night were mighty good," he said. "I think they got the boys quieted down a little. Now how about shootin' enough ducks fer the other camps, too? Might keep the hands on a little longer."

Here was an angle I hadn't figured on. But I knew a bargain when I saw one.

"Tell you what," I said. "I'll get you all the ducks the three camps can eat, with some prairie chickens thrown in. All I ask is my $7 a day, plenty of shells, the old Ford and Barney for my helper."

"Ya got a new job, boy." Big MacKenzie sealed the bargain with a handshake and for the first and only time in my life I was a full-fledged market hunter.

Barney was delighted with the deal. Hunting was a whole lot better than getting a load of straw down your neck. We were up at daybreak the next day.

"Let's just drive around and locate the good spots," I said. Barney was ready for anything that didn't involve pitching bundles. We spent the whole morning rambling around the Bean grain fields. By noon we had twenty chickens in the car and a dozen ducks I had picked up in the smaller potholes.

"Now we'll knock off for today," I said in mid-afternoon. "No use shooting too many birds. The camp can only use so many, and we might shoot ourselves right out of a nice job."

The following morning the weather had cleared and the busy hum of threshing machines again could be heard over the pancake-flat prairies. But Barney and I were professional hunters now and the back-breaking work of a threshing hand was not for us. True to my agreement, we kept the camps supplied with fresh meat, but only enough for one meal at a time.

One frosty morning, just before the season ended, we were sitting in a blind when Barney grabbed my shoulder.

"Look at those big ducks behind us, Jimmy!" he said excitedly.

I swung around in time to see a huge flock of Canadian honkers headed straight for the blind. "Keep down!" I warned. "Those are geese."

But instead of passing over us they crossed to the right of the blind, set their wings and dropped into the marsh. We could see them sitting there, three hundred yards in front of us but as safe as if they had been in the middle of the ocean.

"Only one thing to do," I said. "I'll shoot in the air and when they get up maybe they'll fly within range."

The shot got the birds up, but they merely circled a few times and headed right back into the slough. Just then another flock came in from the fields and in five minutes two more big bunches wheeled down and pitched in with the rest. We sat in amazement and utter futility. There was no way of getting at them.

That night we drove up to the main camp.

"What's the matter now?" MacKenzie asked. "Run out of shells or want yer old job back?"

"Neither," I said. "But have you got any tin around here? I want to make some goose decoys. We spotted a big bunch of honkers today, but the only way to get at 'em is to find where they feed, dig some pits and put out decoys."

By midnight we were back at the bunkhouse with twenty of the roughest looking wood and tin goose silhouettes any hunter ever toted.

At 5 a.m. we headed for the slough in the dark. We had marked an unthreshed grain field a mile from the water where we had seen several flocks of geese feeding the night before. In an hour we had a shallow pit dug, then we set out the decoys and waited . . . and waited.

134

Dick Guptill, one of the last of the old market hunters, tells Roscoe and Gordie Fawcett about the days he killed ducks and geese by the wagon load. The 88-year old veteran is the oldest living Grand American Handicap winner. He won the title at Indianapolis in 1904. He's a fishing guide at Lake Koronis in Minnesota.

Photo by Tommy Lee

Mallards coming in.—Les Kouba

Chicken hunting in Saskatchewan.

Photo by Olive Roberts, Sask. Govt. Photographer

We could hear faintly above the northwest wind the goose talk coming from the marsh. Their excited babble indicated they were getting ready for the morning feed flight. But nothing came over our field.

Toward ten o'clock a small flock got up from the marsh, bucked the wind into the field next to ours, circled twice and sat down . . . safe from the longest reach of my B-B loads. And that was it. Not another bird in the air all day. The sun set and dusk settled down upon the land and I hadn't fired a shot.

Ernie Paynter, game director of Saskatchewan and Herb Moulding of Ducks Unlimited, two of the men who keep a watchful eye over our game birds in Saskatchewan.

But now we knew the geese had switched to a new feed field. Before the next dawn we had another shallow pit dug there. There was a feeling of snow in the night sky and no stars shone through the blackness. Then, as a faint greyness crept upward in the east, snow began to fall, lightly at first and faster as the wind rose. By the time the sky was light enough to see, a raging snowstorm was in progress. Above us in the tangle of whirling snowflakes we could see ducks winging by the thousands before the wind. But not a single goose.

As the morning advanced the whining wind increased and the storm grew into a full-blown blizzard. Somehow I managed to knock down one teal, but the massed flights of bigger ducks were out of range.

"No use staying here," I told Barney. "If this thing gets any worse, we might not make it back to camp at all. And I don't hanker to spend a night out in this stuff."

"I've been ready to go since daylight," said Barney.

How we made it back to the bunkhouse I'll never know. There was no track to guide us and I managed to hold a direction only by keeping the wind quartering at us from our backs.

Suddenly, through the swirling whiteness, I made out a dozen shadowy forms ahead going through the strangest antics I had ever seen. They appeared to be beating the ground with sticks. As we got nearer I recognized several of the harvest hands, each armed with a pitchfork.

They were killing geese with pitchforks. The birds, bewildered by the sudden savagery of the storm, had landed in the bunkhouse yard.

Another crew in the cook shack was plucking ducks, geese and even a few swans as fast as the hands brought them in. Unobtrusively I dropped my scrawny, little teal on a pile of mallards and slipped out of the shack.

The harvest, I knew, was ended with this snowstorm . . . and so was my plush market hunting job.

Before the week was out we were on the train headed back for Winnipeg. I stopped in to report to Grandpa Cruikshank as soon as we got there, and told him how the blizzard had cut short the harvest.

"Whut ya kickin' about?" he asked. "Fer once in yer life ya got all th' duck huntin' ya could stand."

CHAPTER EIGHT

SHOTGUN THRILLS

No one could spend thirty-five years, as I have, covering the Grand American trapshooting tournaments and trap, skeet and live pigeon shoots all over America, Cuba and Europe without meeting and coming to know the great personalities in shotgun shooting. Among them I treasure some of my greatest friendships, yet I still get a thrill out of going to the most insignificant shooting event, whether it be a plain country turkey shoot in Calgary, a live pigeon shoot in Havana, one of Harold Smith's big tournaments in Reno, or a friendly club shoot with Cliff Overvold at Fargo.

I have met all the greats in skeet, trap and live pigeon shooting, and during the early 1920s I talked with many old timers who were able to give me first-hand information on the top gunners of the early days. So a chapter on shotgun shooting could list hundreds of names, if not thousands. But that is not my purpose here.

It seems to me that the great events in trapshooting are the ones to write about. They, in their own spectacular accomplishments, were so remarkable that they have interest for everyone, shooter or not. So here I propose to write briefly about the all-time greatest thrills in shotgun shooting, as I knew them.

I learned much from Fred Kimble, inventor of the choke bore in shotguns and one of the world's greatest duck shots. And I learned much from Fred Gilbert, Spirit Lake, Iowa, one of the greatest of all market hunters. I still have the L. C. Smith shotgun that Fred Kimble gave me a few years ago before he died in California. And in my trophy room is the .22 rifle with which Annie Oakley did most of her exhibition shooting.

A few years ago Bob Peters, a former trapshooter and noted duck hunter, was hunting with me in Manitoba. In a duck blind one day he turned to me and said, "Jimmy, why don't you write a book on your shotgun and rifle experiences? You're the only man left who knows all of the great shots, past and present."

A book on the great events in shooting? Well, it was an idea, and I began going through years of files of shooting records. But when I had done that the list of shooting greats was so long that I realized it would be more effective to write only of the all-time top accomplishments and include them as a chapter in a book of hunting memoirs. These, then, are the things that stand out:

The biggest, most miraculous thing that ever happened in trapshooting was the year of 1938 when Joe Hiestand couldn't miss at the Grand American in Vandalia, Ohio. The Buckeye wizard from Hillsboro, Ohio, took part in every championship and all the preliminaries at the Grand that year. He never missed a target in ten days of firing. He broke 900 straight from sixteen yards, and that didn't include the shoot-offs.

Charlie Ruth of Milwaukee finally could stand it no longer as he watched Joe make ink spots out of the targets. "This is getting monotonous," Charlie remarked. "Even perfection gets on your nerves sometimes."

It should be said to his credit that Joe Hiestand was getting embarrassed about all those targets he was shattering. But after the Grand closed he kept right on shooting and didn't register a miss until he had broken his 1,179th straight target. That was 400 more than Freddie Tomlin's world record long run, and Joe's record still stands today.

Two other remarkable trapshooting performances occur to me, both by youngsters. Nick Egan of New York City and Rufus King, the Texan, both won the roaring Grand handicap when they were fourteen.

Rufus did it first in 1930. His father, Fred King, a world-renowned shot and former champion, was president of the American Trapshooting Association at the time. But his own boy won the prize plum of trapshooting, a title the elder King had been shooting at for more than thirty years.

Young Rufus was too youthful to be frightened when a crowd of 10,000 gathered around the traps to watch him shoot-off with three veterans who, like himself, had broken 97 of 100. He beat them in what was easily the most popular triumph of all time and in one of the most dramatic climaxes I have ever witnessed.

Then there was the unforgettable year of 1954 when young Nick Egan provided the fireworks and scored a darkhorse victory over 2,000 of the world's greatest shots, capturing the Grand American handicap title with 99 of 100 from 19 yards. But chubby young Egan was already a crack shot, so his victory came as no big surprise to his many followers from the big city.

Ned Lilly, at seventeen, was another youngster who attracted worldwide attention when he won everything except the traphouses in the 1933 Grand. That was the year he won the North American clay target championship with 199 of 200 and the class AA crown with the same score.

Beyond that the curly-haired Stanton, Mich., shotgun artist captured the Junior crown with 100 straight and won the high-over-all title with 964 of 1,000, two targets better than Mark Arie and Joe Hiestand turned in. He also tied Walter Beaver for the Grand American title when he broke 98 of 100 from 24 yards. His great work was rewarded later when it became inevitable that I should pick him as captain of my Sports Afield All-America trapshooting team. He still stands in the record as the only Junior shooter ever chosen captain of this team.

Another outstanding all-time great performance was turned in by Joan Pfleuger, the young girl from Florida whose father, Al, is the famed Miami taxidermist. At seventeen she was the feminine shooting star of the 1950 Grand. Then she went out and won the coveted Champion of Champions race, breaking 100 straight and defeating the great Ned Lilly, Mercer Tennille, Dean Blank and Hugh Crossen in the shoot-off. Tennille was merely the greatest doubles shooter of all time.

I have watched some dramatic shotgun exhibitions in my time, and one I'll never forget was in that same year of 1950 when Rudy

Joe Hiestand and Fred Tomlin at the Grand American. Tomlin came to the 1938
Grand American Trapshoot with a long-run record of 766 straight targets. But
Joe was hot that week and ran up a string of 1,179 straight, a new record which
still stands.

Photo by W. P. Mayfield

Lela Hall Frank has won the
National Women's championship seven times.

Photo by Fritz Howell, AP

Trapshooting Queens Glorida Mapes Kraemer and Evelyn Primm.

CAPTAINS OF SPORTS AFIELD
ALL-AMERICA TRAPSHOOTING TEAMS

1931—Steve Crothers,
        Pennsylvania

1932—Steve Crothers,
        Pennsylvania

1933—Ned Lilly, Michigan

1934—Joe Hiestand, Ohio

1935—Joe Hiestand, Ohio

1936—Joe Hiestand, Ohio

1937—Hale Jones, Illinois

1938—Joe Hiestand, Ohio

1939—Phil Miller, Indiana

1940—Vic Reinders, Wisconsin

1941—Vic Reinders, Wisconsin

1942—Julius Petty, Arkansas

1943—Herschel Cheek, Indiana

1944—Vic Reinders, Wisconsin

1945—Rudy Etchen, Tennessee

1946—Mercer Tennille, Louisiana

1947—Joe Hiestand, Ohio

1948—Ed Castanedo, Louisiana

1949—Joe Hiestand, Ohio

1951—Arnold Riegger,
        Washington

1952—Arnold Riegger,
        Washington

1953—Rudy Etchen, Idaho

1954—Arnold Riegger,
        Washington

1955—Arnold Riegger,
        Washington

1956—Ned Lilly, Michigan

1957—Dan Orlich, Nevada

1958—Vic Reinders, Wisconsin

Vic Reinders, Captain of the 1958 Sports Afield All-America trapshooting team, buys a belt from Ed Scherer at the Grand American. Scherer averaged .9970 at skeet in 1957, to set a new world's record.

Photo by W. P. Mayfield

Iva Pembridge Jarvis, the famous woman trapshooter. Lela Hall Frank and Iva are the two greatest amateur Women trapshooters of all times.

Photo by W. P. Mayfield

Etchen, the Sun Valley shooting instructor, broke the first 100 straight doubles at the Grand. Then he walked away with the high-over-all championship by the unprecedented, all-time record score of 980 of 1,000 on mixed handicaps, doubles and 16-yard birds.

Over the years Iva Pembridge Jarvis and Lela Hall Frank stand alone as the two greatest amateur women trapshots of all time. They provided thrill after thrill for spectators everywhere. Lela, the Californian, has won the North American clay target championship no less than seven times. Iva, a Phillipsburg, Kan., school teacher, won the big Reno, Nev., handicap over both men and women when she shattered 99 of 100 from 22 yards for a victory that netted her $3,500.

For one hour's work that wasn't bad, and certainly more than she made in a year of teaching school.

Among the greatest of Canadian trap stars is the youthful George Genereaux of Saskatoon. This transplanted hockey and baseball star won the world's trapshooting championship at Helsinki, Finland in 1952. He was Canada's only gold medal winner.

147

CHAPTER NINE

Pheasant Hunting

Because he is so gaudy to look at, so crafty in the field and so delicious on the table, the Chinese ringneck pheasant is one of America's most popular upland game birds. Hunting estimates place the nation's total annual bag of pheasants at something in the neighborhood of 15,000,000 birds. Only the dove hunter downs more, which makes Mr. Chink No. 2 in the popularity poll of our nimrods.

There are other cogent reasons for the pheasant's popularity among the millions of scattergunners. One is the fact that he is so widely distributed. Pheasants are found in about thirty northern states, from New England to Washington and Oregon, from Minnesota to Missouri. Another is the bird's habitat preference for the cultivated acres of man. Wherever corn is raised, there you are likely to find pheasants.

Few game birds are more adaptable to the fluctuations of weather, and few are hardier in the face of unfavorable climactic conditions. So, even in their years of greatest adversity, there are always some pheasants surviving for the hunters of the next season.

Among all the states that support ringnecks, South Dakota, with no stocking at all other than the original plantings, has become the acknowledge pheasant capital of the nation. In the peak pheasant year of 1944 South Dakota had an estimated population of 16,000,000 ringnecks, and the next year 200,000 hunters, including 86,000 non-residents, bagged 7,500,000 birds in the state.

That's a great tribute to a bird that was only introduced from China in 1880 and provided Oregon with the first pheasant season in America in 1893.

The fact that the pheasant is both weather and disease resistant is one reason why he has survived in this new country of his adoption. His present range extends well north into Alberta, where winters really get tough. Snow and cold he can stand, but sleet and blizzards have been his undoing in some local areas where re-stocking was necessary the following year.

He likes and must have the winter cover of sloughs and marshes, wild hay meadows and brush patches, but this should be close to feed, with corn, soybeans, clover, weed seeds and alfalfa rating high on his list. In spring his food preferences are cut worms, crop pests and insects, but as summer advances he varies his diet with wild grapes, berries and fruit-bearing plants. When the crops are matured in the fall he leans heavily on corn, and his winter fare consists predominantly of weed seeds.

During the fall hunting season Mr. Ringneck's day will run about like this: He'll be abroad at sunup, leaving his roosting cover in the alfalfa, meadows or slough-grass marshes to move out for food. If corn is available, he'll head for that, or for a soybean field, or perhaps along the edge of barley or other small grain stubble to pick up leavings of the combines.

Late in the morning he'll have enough of feeding and head for handy resting cover—some vine-grown tangle, or back to the cattail marsh, or in the densest underbrush he can find. If it has a dusting spot, so much the better, for he likes to dust himself at noon. And preferably there should be water at hand—a creek, a side-hill spring, a little pool in a slough will do.

In mid-afternoon, out he comes again for another feed. This he'll top off with a few minutes of graveling along a roadside to grind up the corn in his crop. Then, as the blue shadows of evening envelop the land, you'll see him sailing across the fields back to his roosting spot.

With this routine in mind, the pheasant hunter can plan his day most advantageously. He'll be close to roosting cover at daybreak (assuming that morning shooting is legal, as it is not in some states). He'll move into the cornfields or the alfalfa and soybean patches as the birds move into them to feed. He'll hunt the densest cover at noon and return to the fields in the afternoon.

But wherever he hunts he'll always find that the pheasant's craftiness and unpredictability make him more than a competent adversary. His perverse habits have unstrung more than one experienced upland gunner.

"Habits!" grunted my friend Ray Mithun on a South Dakota pheasant hunting trip we made one year. "The only habits these birds have are bad.

"They won't sit for a dog. They run ahead of you and around you in the cornfields. Or they get up out of range when you just rustle a cornstalk. Or they sit tight and let you walk right by them."

He was so right. Pheasants do all of these things—and more. The big, cowardly roosters always let the hens explore ahead first, always let them flush first. Then, if the coast is clear, they proceed. So if a hen roars up in front of you, get yourself set—there's probably a rooster nearby.

The most popular and probably the most effective method of hunting pheasants is the drive. This is particularly useful in large cornfields where they congregate during morning and afternoon feeding periods. The hunting group may consist of any number of guns from four up to fifteen or twenty. South Dakota by law limits pheasant hunting parties to twelve. But generally the larger the cornfield selected to hunt, the more drivers you will need to flush the birds and prevent them from circling behind the driving line.

It's always prudent to select a drive captain and then let him make the assignments so the greatest coordination may be obtained. His first job is to determine the direction of the drive, and this will usually be into the wind because that is the direction in which pheasants flush. On downwind drives birds often flush behind the gunners and after they've passed.

Ready to be released—Pheasants at Spring Lake Game Farm at Eau Claire, Wis.

Pheasant hunting in western Minnesota with Blix Donnelley, left, St. Louis Cardinal baseball pitcher and world's series hero in 1944 and Rosy Ryan, right, former big league pitcher.

The captain also will name the hunters who are to drive and those who will post at the other end of the field to take birds flushing out of range ahead of the drivers. The best shots, or those least able to walk, are generally assigned to the posting task. They'll station themselves a little more than a gun range apart at the end of the field toward which the drivers will work. Here the birds will be concentrated as the drivers approach, and if all goes according to Hoyle, they'll flush at about the same time within range of both drivers and posters.

At a signal from the captain, the drivers start walking, strung out in a half-moon formation no more than six to eight corn rows apart. The end men should be twenty paces or so ahead of the middle of the line to be in a more favorable position to take birds flushing out the sides of the drivers.

If the field is too large to cover entirely in one sweep, the drivers merely move over one lap, or the breadth of their drive, and take it back to their starting point. Sooner or later the whole field will be covered and usually the birds will be concentrated in the last corner to be covered.

"What a pheasant hunter needs most is a good pair of legs," says Paul Schmitt, with whom I have worked on innumerable drives in South Dakota and southwestern Minnesota. That's readily understood when you realize that some drives work a half-mile-long cornfield three or four times before it is combed clean.

Another highly productive method of hunting pheasants is with birds dogs, pointers or setters, or with a trailing and flushing dog like the springer spaniel. But this, of necessity, limits the hunting party to three or four guns, because no dog will work well in the midst of a dozen or so hunters. His master's orders are lost in the confusion of a large group.

Use of one or more dogs also limits the type of cover that may be hunted. Since pheasants will not hold for a dog in cornfields, but run instead, the pointing breeds are out. I've seen many a good bird dog confused, frustrated and spoiled by working him on pheasants in corn. Even springers, whose purpose is to trail and flush running birds, have their limitations in corn. Trained to work close to the gun in heavy cover, they will be tempted to range out far and wide for a bird running fast down a clear corn row.

154

If you must hunt corn with dogs, my suggestion is to use a retriever. Keep him at heel during the drive and cast him out only after a bird has been flushed and downed. That's his purpose, to retrieve, and thus he is particularly adapted to work in corn. In such open cover crippled birds often travel far and would be lost without the help of retrieving breeds like Labradors, Chesapeakes and golden retrievers.

This is not to say that German shorthaired pointers, English pointers and setters, or springer spaniels have no place in pheasant hunting. They distinctly do, but in the right type of cover. In the marshes, uncut clover or alfalfa fields, wild hay meadows, slough grass patches and along brushy ditches the pointing and trailing breeds work well. That's because the birds hold better for dogs in heavy cover, or if they run they don't run far.

Some of the best pheasant hunting I've ever had was with Johnny and Jackie Moran, the All-American trapshooters from Indianapolis and Johnny's good pointing dog. The keen nose of that dog would put us on birds in places you'd swear no self-respecting pheasant would try to use for hiding. We found them in tufts of hay left by the mower, tufts no bigger than a card table. We found them in weed-grown rock piles in the center of open plowing. And in almost coverless ditches right beside a main highway. Without a good pointing dog most hunters would have passed up such spots as barren of game.

The choice of shotgun, bore and shot size has always been a widely debated subject among pheasant hunters. True enough, the little 20-gauge with light No. 8 skeet loads has downed its share of birds—in the hands of the expert. But it's my contention that the average pheasant hunter, who gets out only once or twice a year, then stores his gun away until next season, wants all the pattern he can get. And he needs considerably more energy behind each pellet than light trap and skeet loads will give him.

Remember, the pheasant is a large and fat bird in late fall, and he can absorb considerable lead without rolling over dead. Witness the number of birds that are crippled and lost each season. My own guess, after years of watching it happen, is that for every two birds the average pheasant hunter puts in his bag, he loses the third as a cripple.

So he wants all the pattern he can get, and the densest pattern in a 30-inch circle at thirty yards is put there by a 12-gauge shotgun.

That's because you obviously can crowd more pellets, No. 6 for example, into a 12-gauge shell than into a 20-gauge case. But why No. 6 shot for pheasants, you ask? Because it's the happiest compromise between No. 4 loads, which are large with a big wallop but fewer pellets, and No. 7½, which are small with a lighter sock but many pellets.

Let's settle, then, on the 12-gauge shotgun with standard No. 6 game loads for the average pheasant hunter. If he wants to cut it really fine, he could use high base 7½ loads in the early part of the season, when the birds are younger, less feathered out and smaller. And No. 4 loads toward the end of the season when pheasants are bigger, carry a heavier load of fat and flush wilder. But 6's will do the job from beginning to end if you want an all-purpose, all-season load.

Now about choke. The arguments rage here, too. But consider that most pheasants are shot under twenty-five yards of range. At this distance a full-choked barrel would make hamburger out of a pheasant if the gunner is dead on. That's one count against the full choke.

Furthermore, the average two-trip pheasant hunter is seldom dead on. He doesn't shoot his gun enough to achieve that kind of accuracy. So he needs a little more spread, and a modified choke will give him just that. Dan McInnis, manager of the St. Anthony Gun Club, one of the best pheasant gunners in my book, has this to say about choke:

"The average upland gunner isn't good enough to use a full choke. And he isn't quick enough to use an open bore, with which he could take his game under twenty yards. So I say the modifed choke is the ticket for pheasants."

Length of the barrel makes absolutely no practical difference as to range in pheasant shooting, but it makes a whale of a difference in the speed of the swing while getting "on" the bird. Most gunners use 30-inch barrels, and these are fine in duck hunting where you have time to get on the target. But they leave something to be desired where a quick swing is necessary, as in upland gunning.

My choice would be 28-inch barrels. Make them improved cylinder and modified if you're using a double, or modified if you have but one barrel. You can swing twenty-eight inches of barrel right handily, and for close-up work on pheasants it's speed of swing that counts.

Hitting them is something else again. You've got to convince yourself that about one-third of a pheasant is tail, and hitting them

156

Henry Davis, world's greatest hunting dog authority, field trial judge and author.

there doesn't bring home any meat. As soon as you've learned that you'll start shooting for the head where your aim ought to be. And thus you'll be centering the vital part of the bird in your shot pattern.

At the relatively close ranges pheasants are shot, with most birds going straight away or quartering away, you've got to get right on them quickly. Keep the gun swinging with them until the muzzle covers the head and pull the trigger as the muzzle passes the head. Then you'll be downing birds consistently.

Such a shooting method automatically provides the right lead, even on right angle birds. Don't let anybody tell you to lead a pheasant one foot, two feet or six feet. There are too many variables to be precise about the amount of lead. These include wind, speed of the bird, distance from the gunner, angle of flight, dampness content of the shells and even the temperament of the hunter.

Just get the muzzle of your gun on the bird, no matter how he's flying, swing it up to the head and "pull" as you swing past. You'll come home with your share.

We mentioned temperament. That's something pheasants take advantage of. Their raucous, booming flush has unnerved many an upland gunner. Then, startled, he pokes the gun at the fast diminishing bird and lets fly in the general direction. Of course, he misses, shoots behind. He was never "on it" at all.

The thing to cultivate is the calm, completely self-controlled attitude. That can come with experience, and it can come with a conscious effort of will. As you walk in pheasant cover keep the gun always at ready, with the right hand covering the trigger guard, the left on the fore-end and the gun pointed upward at a 45-degree angle.

Resolve to be in control of each step you make and each movement of arms, head and eyes. Be alert, but not jumpy. Relaxed alertness does it. When you do have to make a move, don't leap into it, but swing into it with a continuing, rhythmic motion and let the motion follow through to its conclusion.

That is what is known as good timing in wing shooting. You've got to make it a habit, by will power or experience, before you can call yourself a consistently good pheasant shot.

As for clothes in pheasant hunting, the lighter they are the better.

You'll be walking a lot and you don't want to be burdened with heavy stuff. Close weave duck pants that won't snag but still are light, and a lightweight hunting jacket are indicated. Footwear should be as light as possible, too, so you won't be dragging your feet when you come in. Bird hunter boots with nine-inch tops are fine, but for a really light-footed feeling try a pair of canvas basketball shoes.

When you've bagged your pheasant, getting the bird home in good condition is something to consider. All animal tissue begins to deteriorate from the moment of death, and the process of decomposition is accelerated by heat. The focal point of heat in all game is the body cavity where the internal organs are housed.

If you really want to keep your birds fresh, it's well to open them with a knife at the vent and remove entrails, lungs, heart and other organs while still in the field. Then the body cavity is cooled quickly and the meat stays fresh.

But if this seems like too much of a burden, although it shouldn't be, the very least you can do is to keep the birds separated in your car going home. The way to assure a "high" taste in the birds when they are cooked is to dump them in a heap in a corner of your car trunk, and then make the long drive home without any air getting to them so they can cool.

As for cooking, there are dozens of excellent recipes for preparing pheasant, and in the book of many gourmets there is no finer game. But why not leave it to the little lady at home, who does all the cooking for you anyway? By now she should know how to please your palate.

Then, as you sit at your table stuffing yourself with the fine, white breast of a pheasant, you can offer a vote of thanks to a bird that challenges your nerves, stamina, shooting eye and reaction time.

Fortunately for all of us, this crafty creature is likely to be with us a long, long while.

CHAPTER TEN

GUIDES make the DIFFERENCE

Friend, philosopher, father confessor and amateur psychiatrist are what you expect your guide to be. The doggonedest thing is—that's what most of them are

From Cabo Blanco's Black Marlin to Kodiak's brown bear, bagging the quarry you seek is much more than 50 per cent dependent on your guide. He's the lad with the power to make or break your party. The wonder is, with all the tyro expects of his guide, that anyone in his right mind would take up the profession.

Your guide must be a friend, philosopher, father confessor, amateur psychiatrist. He should be cheerful, alert, calm, unruffled. He must be courteous. He ought to have a sense of humor. Yet you want him simple, an unaffected man, but one who can spin a yarn deftly. He should be capable of quick decisions, but remain pliable; talkative without boring, modest but confident.

All of which is slightly more than you'd expect of your mother-in-law, the President or the family doctor.

It's said the best guides are born with a canoe paddle in one hand and an ax in the other. Yours must know outboard-motor repairs, gin rummy and poker, weather signs, cooking in the rain, first aid, backpacking and compass reading. Above all, he should know where fish are, when and what they want; the cover game prefers, how to get at it and what to do about packing it home once your unerring eye has brought it down.

No wonder a guide is such an important person. The saddening thing is so few people realize it. Many of us owe our lives to a guide, yet regard him as something between a draft horse and a valet.

Not me. To this day I'll never forget my debt to Howard Thompson, a guide at Calvert's Camp on Lake of the Woods.

With the late Robert Page Lincoln, we started out from camp one day with two heavily laden canoes, bound for two weeks of fishing. We crossed over the old Indian portage to Crow Lake, then worked our way to Sioux Narrows, camping out each night. Finally we headed across the Big Traverse of Whitefish Bay on our way back to meet a party of fishermen from Chicago.

Halfway across the bay a sudden and terrific storm blew up. Waves nearly six feet high bore down on us. Alone in the towed canoe I was scared stiff. I glanced ahead to Howard, looking for reassurance. He was outwardly calm. Seeing me clinging to both gunwales with a vise-like grip, he shouted back:

"Pretty rough. Better take off your boots and lie flat on the floor of the canoe. I think we can make it to shore."

He thinks! I knew then I should have stayed home. I was less confident when he threw out our two grub boxes. Finally he removed the outboard and laid it in the bottom of his canoe. Pitching and tossing on the floor of my own craft, my racing thoughts embraced the comforts of wife and fireside. "If I ever get back from this one I'll never go fishing again," I told myself. Each roll of the canoe seemed its last.

We drifted with the wind maybe an hour. But it was eternity for me as I waited out every breathless moment, listening for the sound of the canoe scraping the gravel shore. Then the wind died as suddenly as it had risen. We paddled in to a rocky, inhospitable shore, but it looked like paradise to me. I glanced at Lincoln. His face was drawn in an ash-white mask.

"The rest of my life I'll owe to a guide," he said.

Knowing what to do in an emergency is so important that the Saskatchewan Government is now conducting a school for guides at Lac La Ronge. They're taught all the ramifications of good guiding, from starting a balky outboard to administering artificial respiration.

In many provinces and some states guides are licensed. They have to pass rigid examinations to qualify. Alaska, for instance, has at least 140 registered guides who have proved themselves capable of handling any emergency and getting you back alive. Wisconsin has nearly 1,000. In some states the guides themselves have formed voluntary associations with qualifications for membership that weed out incompetents.

The important thing in all guiding, of course, is to get you to good game cover or fishing water, give you your chance and get you back. Guides have given their lives in pursuit of this goal. It's one of the hazards of the profession. Who would know better than Rod Ducharme?

Rod is a French-Canadian guide who weighs 275 pounds and runs a duck hunting layout on the Delta Marsh at the south end of Lake Manitoba. One blustery October daybreak he came rattling up to our own duck club in his broken-down truck. He announced, "Cheemy, da seelver cans, she is in!" Of course, he meant the big drake silver canvasbacks' last flight into the marsh each fall.

He might have said, "In two minutes an H-bomb will fall here." We got into action that quick. Stan Bentham, the Winnipeg Free Press outdoor expert, was throwing shells into his duffel bag and hauling on his parka before I had my gun off the rack. We piled into the truck and headed back for Rod's shack at St. Ambroise. The wind was veering to the northwest and increasing to gale force. Ice film had already formed around the edges of the marsh. We had to break through it to get out to one of the islands where there was some open water. A dozen big, silver-breasted cans were there, bobbing in the hills and valleys of the white-tipped waves. They beat their way out upwind at our approach, but they came zooming back by twos and threes. In an hour we had five down.

Then the weather really got rough, with snow slating in and ice making up fast in our blinds of rushes. We knew it would be suicide to stay longer.

"She's gon' get worse," said Rod. "We better hit f'r home mighty queek!"

Stan and I started out in one duckboat, leaving the decoys for Rod to pick up. We had a mile to go, but it might have been a hundred, for all we could see of the obliterated shore line. The waves out in open water seemed at least three feet high, and they broke into the boat, drenching us to our long-johns.

Photo by Bruce Reinecker

Leo Flammand, trapper and commercial fisherman, has been one of our duck guides for nineteen years. He guides fishermen at Barney Lamm's Ball Lake lodge in Ontario during the summer.

Pete Burton, God's Lake, Manitoba, "ace" fishing guide and trapper.

Pat Hemingway, African white-hunter, received his early training from Papa Hemingway, one of the greatest hunters of our time. Pat's first big game trophy, a mule deer, was shot in the Shoshone mountains at Sun Valley, Idaho. Papa Hemingway was as proud as youthful Pat. Pat was my guide in Africa.

Then I snapped an oar. The boat immediately swung broadside to the waves, helpless as a feather in a tornado. We were at the mercy of the gale, and the future looked dark. I glanced around and saw the dim outline of Rod's boat quartering down on us from the windward. There never was a more welcome sight, and I shouted myself hoarse for help.

Rod saw our plight at once. The thing to do was to get a line to our boat and tow it downwind to keep the waves from boarding us. When he had worked his way upwind of us, he half-raised up so he could reverse his rowing position to tow us. But the center of gravity of his craft was too high, loaded as it was with bags of heavy canvasback decoys. A wave caught him and over he went. The decoy bags floated off on the wind and Rod's empty duckboat now bobbed like a cork off down the wind.

Now our situation was critical. We were powerless to go to his aid, and our water-burdened boat itself couldn't last much longer. I remember wondering who'd be the first to find our bodies. Then I saw Rod working his way toward us by treading water and clawing dog-fashion with his arms. He finally reached the transom. Stan grabbed his wrist and started to help him aboard.

"No," Rod yelled. "The boat cannot take me. I weel hold on. Paddle for shore, Cheemy, queek."

It didn't occur to me until later why Rod didn't swim back to his own boat. He knew with only one oar we'd be powerless to control our boat and would soon swamp broadside in the waves. His body, hanging at the stern acted as a drag and allowed the waves to push us forward.

But how he survived the icy water on the long and frenzied tramp across the marsh I'll never know. Except that guides are a hardy breed. They can endure tests beyond the realm of mere mortals. But Rod Ducharme nearly gave his life for two hunters that day on the marsh.

Of all the guides I have met, I'm ready to admit now that the job of the White Hunter guide in Africa is the toughest—and the most dangerous. Nothing could be more exacting than his 12-hour day, week after week, year after year, in country few men can stand up to for more than a short period. His fund of knowledge about game, weather and terrain must be tremendous; he must be always on the alert to see that his safari guests don't stumble, through ignorance, into making even the smallest error. Errors in Africa can be fatal.

I got my indoctrination into the rigors of White Hunter guiding the past winter when I went on a 14-day safari in Tanganyika with Pat Hemingway, son of the famous novelist Ernest Hemingway, whom I have known for more years than either of us like to admit. Pat learned his hunting and fishing from his father, but he was so intrigued by the country and the White Hunter's life in Africa that he decided to spend the rest of his life there.

Now he's considered one of the best safari guides on the Dark Continent. Since I left Africa Pat has formed his new safari with his headquarters at Arusha. He's gone further in the studious pursuit of his profession than any man I know. His library is full of books on African game birds and animals. He has, on his own, made exhaustive studies of each. Hunting with him was a liberal education, and he imparted his knowledge far beyond the call of duty of the average guide I had known before.

My ambition, long before flying to Africa, had been to lay low a well-maned lion. Pat Hemingway completely sympathized with this desire, and for twelve long days he spent countless hours putting out lion baits only to see the jackals and hyenas lay waste to them. Therein I discovered another virtue of guides in general and Pat in particular. He had the patience of a saint.

But even on him the days of driving his British Land-Rover around mountains, across rivers and over stones began to tell. In his eyes was the exhaustion of being ever alert for even the faintest sign of my elusive lion. He stopped often to chatter in several dialects with native bands, and therein I discovered another requirement of the African White Hunter. He must be able to converse fluently in several tongues, something required of few other guides.

So there we were, reeling across the vast Serengeti Plains looking for my lion, and I knew Pat was tired. Yet he missed no detail of the terrain ahead as the rest of us dozed in the back of his machine.

Suddenly, three females got up immediately ahead and to the left. His eyes glued on the animals, Pat swerved to the right to avoid plowing into them and the Land-Rover crashed against a tree. We were stalled in a situation pregnant with danger and the lions less than 35 yards away.

"Don't shoot!" Pat warned. "They're females."

The lions eyed us casually. Then they simply melted into the high grass rolling away from our scene of distress. Greenhorns that we were, we, the hunters, breathed easier.

Pat merely got out, cut a small tree and pried the truck out of a hole at the foot of the larger tree we had hit. Then he shifted into reverse, backed away and we were off again.

"Anyone get any gray hairs over that one?" A smile was spreading across his amiable face. "It happens every day in the life of the White Hunter."

What do guides do for a living when they aren't guiding? Most of them are trappers or lumberjacks or commercial fishermen. But I have known guides who were farmers, prospectors, forest rangers, game wardens, even schoolteachers. The one thing they all had in common was a consuming love of the outdoors and a profound knowledge of nature in all its aspects—the wild, the dangerous, the benign.

Such a man was Pete Burton, trapper on the remotest stretches of God's River in northeastern Manitoba. I knew him only slightly when I made my first flying trip into God's Lake with Barney Lamm. Barney operates a fishing camp on Ball Lake north of Kenora, Ontario, with side trips to God's for speckled trout and lake trout. After three days out with Pete I was convinced no other man would live long enough to learn all Pete knows about this mighty watercourse. He had studied and fished every riffle; he could pinpoint each rock and tell you whether you'd catch a "spec" in the eddy behind it. He was tuned to its moods, from anger to babbling happiness.

So we were tied up, Pete and I, at the bottom of a white-water rapids and I cast to a likely eddy back of a rock under an outreaching alder. The hit was immediate. The fish came slicing toward the canoe as I took up line. Before I could lift the fish into the canoe Pete was shaking his head.

"That's the small one. Only weigh about three pounds. Let him go and try again. There's a five-pounder in there."

He was right. Two casts later I had Mr. Big on. After the excitement of the battle and the victory, we weighed him on the spring scales in my tackle box. The indicator stopped at just a shade over five pounds.

"Pete," I said, "I'll bet you've got a name for every spec in this river. And for the rock each one hides behind."

The guide grinned. "I dunno. But I guess I could tell you what water you'd be wasting your time in and where you're going to catch the big one."

On the way back upstream, in the quiet stretches, I got to thinking. Here was a man who had guided General Mark Clark, Dr. Charles Mayo, Gerry Malahar, Hugh Grey, Jack Cornelius, Dallas Gordon Rupe, Don Dickey, Walter Baskerville—the famous and the wealthy. I wondered aloud what would happen if someone offered him a $10,000 job in Chicago.

"Well, I made $1,000 last winter on fur," he said. "That's more'n I need. I get all the trout and caribou and moose meat me and my family can eat. I got a snug house on Elk Island in God's Lake. That $10,000 wouldn't make me any happier."

Pressure. Pete doesn't know the word. For that matter, I've never met a guide who ever got himself bedded down with a heart attack. Even the clothes for Pete's family are simply acquired. His wife makes them out of caribou and moose hides. And he has his own private hunting preserve—a registered trap line 75 miles long, 20 miles wide. Its 1,500 square miles are far larger and more abundantly supplied with game than Dick Mellon's 36,000-acre Rolling Rock hunting preserve in Pennsylvania, a layout on which millions have been spent.

Seldom does the guide appear at a disadvantage in his native cover, but I once had the pleasure of getting the laugh on an old-timer named J. O. Sabin, who guided President Theodore Roosevelt when he was Governor of New York State and went with him to Africa in 1909.

J. O. had a theory about deer hunting that was interesting, if not completely comfortable. As he put it:

"I developed this here theory in Texas in 1927, before the ranchers began to sell deer tracks and charge $100 to see them in the dust."

It seems he was trying out a new scope, an old Weaver 29S. So on the way out to post for a buck he shot a skunk to try the scope. It worked fine, so he let the skunk lay under a mesquite tree, because a deer drive was on. Pretty soon he saw a buck, a doe and a fawn coming on the run with a brisk wind blowing from him to the deer.

When they got to the skunk they stopped, looked around, and the buck reared up on his hind legs and began pawing at the skunk. Not hitting it, mind you, just pawing around it. They were less than 50

169

Jelley Smith is still a great musky guide. He holds a 45-pound musky caught by Harry Johnston on one of our trips to Eagle Lake in Ontario.

Photo by Maurice Florance

Doug Cameron, one of Canada's greatest pilots, acts as my guide at Elk Island, God's Lake, Manitoba.

General Mark Clark, Dr. Charles Mayo, Don Dickey, Jack Cornelius, Hugh Grey, Walter Baskerville, and other famous sportsmen have bedded down in Pete Burton's trappers' shack to fish God's River with him.

yards away with the wind blowing from J. O. to them, yet they gave him plenty of time to bear the scope down on the buck and let off a shot. That convinced the hunter that skunk scent had disguised his own rich aroma. So the next day he went to the same spot, rubbed his boots against the dead skunk and took up his stand again. He got another deer, despite the same adverse wind.

Years later when I met him, J. O. was still swearing by skunk oil for deer hunting. So I made a date to go out for deer with him and give it a try. He was then living at Dalbo, Minnesota, doing odd jobs, selling an occasional batch of skunk oil and living on his memories.

Came the eve of the hunt and I arrived in Dalbo with high hopes. But, as I drove down the single street of the little hamlet, I began to smell skunk. When I stopped in front of Sabin's house it was so rank I had to hold my nose. J. O. came out with the look of a man who had just swallowed a glass of clabbered milk by mistake.

"Wife wouldn't let me keep the skunk oil on the porch," he said. "So I put it up on the roof. Wind came along and blew the jar off and it smashed to smithereens on the sidewalk. Now she's made me bury my huntin' clothes and I don't think I kin go with you."

The thing to do when out with a guide is remember he's a man of equal stature with yourself—not a machine, not a doormat. Humility in your unfamiliar surroundings wins his respect, for the guide's chief abomination is the know-it-all who insists on guiding the guide. Runner-up to this pest is the tippler, who comes not to fish or hunt, but to get his nose wet and keep it that way. Third on the black list is the wild caster who's always hanging his bait up in trees or catching it in the guide's shirt on the back swing. But I would rate modesty as the patron's chief asset, and it pays rich dividends.

I learned this lesson in guide relationship while hunting the Louisiana marshes with Major Jim Brown, then game and fish director of the state. Nobody had been getting any geese, and the old Negro guide Major Brown assigned to me looked too sleepy to give me a chance to upset the status quo. So, when he cranked up the marsh buggy and headed out across the rushes, I tried to engage him in conversation about where the birds might be. Sam wasn't buying it. I switched the subject to his family and his kids back home.

That softened him a little, but when we'd gone 12 miles out in the marsh without seeing a goose, I began to wonder if I'd got to him. Sam stopped at a barren mud flat surrounded by marsh water and bog. It didn't have the look of goose country, but I kept my mouth shut.

Sam climbed out on the flat and began collecting clumps of dried mud. Then he took an old newspaper from his hip pocket and started folding sheets of the paper around each clump, twisting one of the free corners upward to form a goose neck. When he had set up 24 of these makeshift decoys he got back in the marsh buggy and pushed it into some nearby rushes.

"Don't yuh-all worry, Mistuh Jimmy. I been savin' this heah spot for sumpin' special. Watch me coax 'em with this heah ol' paper."

In a few minutes the distant honking of snow geese came to us faintly. Soon we could see the V of their formation against a skim-milk sky. They came straight in, confident and trusting, without so much as a whisper of a call from us. I had time to get two geese down with the first volley, reload and down two more. Then I looked at Sam and an ear-to-ear smile was creasing his shiny face.

"Mistuh Jimmy," he said, "you done good. Hain't everybody Majah Brown brings down heah I woulda showed this spot to."

It was a case of where a little humility, plus a little interest in a guide's personal problems paid off.

But, of course, you've been in the country before. You know what you're after and how to go about getting it. So why a guide? You could save money and it might be more fun to go it alone, do your own cooking, camp making and hunting or fishing.

Unfortunately, the average hunter or fisherman, whose business isn't hunting and fishing, doesn't have time enough to gain the experience he needs for the greatest success on his outings. So he provides himself with an expert who can save him from wasting time looking were game and fish aren't. There's the real value of your guide.

Personally, I'd never be caught away from home without one. They'll make the difference between success and failure—if you'll let them.

Fred Alford, Dallas, Texas, skeet shooter and sportsman. Mr. Alford and several other Dallas sportsmen were responsible for the new $250,000 Dallas gun club, the finest in the world. Fred Alford has done more to cement friendly relations with the Puerto Rican government and sportsmen than any other American.

Photo by Merle Hereford

CHAPTER ELEVEN

Skeet Personalities

Each year the sport of skeet shooting has become more popular, which is a tribute to the game since it dates back only to about 1915 when it was originated at the old Glen Rock Kennels of Andover, Mass.

There a group of upland game shooters, principally the late Bill Foster and C. E. Davis with his son Henry W., used to shoot at clay targets to obtain wingshot practice. They were the inventors of skeet.

The sport caught on like a prairie fire, and today the game is well organized from one end of the nation to the other. Club and zone shoots and a National Skeet Tournament are held each year. I visited and handled publicity for the first National Skeet Championships at Cleveland, Ohio, in 1935.

That year L. S. Pratt of Indianapolis won the all-gauge crown with 244 of 250. Harold Russell, a top skeet and trap shooter from Minneapolis, carried off professional honors with 97 of 100. Skeet scores were low in those days and shooters few in number. So those winning 1935 scores have special significance. Today skeet gunners equal the top performances of trapshooters.

Carola Mandel, the Cuban beauty from Chicago, provided one of the greatest skeet performances in my recollection. It was at Waterford, Mich., in 1954. This brilliant shooter won the National 20-gauge Open

Olita Alford, (right) tells how she broke the world's .410 skeet record at the Reno Nationals in 1956. Listening are youthful Judy Allen, Captain of the Women's All-America Skeet team and Betty Ragland. Betty fired 825 shots in a shoot-off for the National Handicap title at Dallas against Johnny Pachmayr, the famous Los Angeles gunsmith. The race ended in a tie.

Carola Mandel, Queen of Skeet, the National high average skeet gunner in 1956 with .9940 on 1,200 targets, and 1954 National 20-gauge skeet champion. No other woman skeet shooter has ever won a national championship competing with men.

Championship with 100 straight hits, then broke 50 straight in the shoot-off to defeat four male marksmen.

She became the first woman skeet shooter in history to win the National Open title. And the remarkable part of it was she won with a fractured ankle, which she had broken the night before. After that performance Chet Crites of Detroit, a former national skeet champion, remarked to George White, general manager of the National, "It's no disgrace getting beat by Carola. She's the best."

In 1956 this talented shotgun star again gained nationwide recognition when she led both men and women high average shooters of America with the remarkable average of .9940 on 1,200 targets.

There was a time back in 1941 when Jean Smythe, a terrific little 95-pound competitor from Palm Beach, Fla., electrified the shotgun fans at Indianapolis as she broke 100 straight to tie S. L. Hutcheson of New York for the National 20-gauge Open Skeet ittle.

Now Judy Allen, the Oakland, Calif., college student, is one of the women skeet greats. She broke 150 straight in the main event and then 75 straight in a hair-raising shoot-off to win the California Ladies' Championship over Thelma Anguish, another great shot from Pacomia.

In 1956, Mrs. Fred "Olita" Alford of Dallas, Texas, scored one of the big upsets in skeet at Reno when she broke 96 of 100 to win the National Women's Subsmall crown. This was three targets better than the then world record.

Betty Ragland, another famous woman shooter from Dallas, competed in a world record marathon shoot-off with Johnny Pachmayr, the Los Angeles gunsmith, when they fired 825 shots to end up in a tie. That was the year the spectacular Ann Hecker of Tucson, Ariz., racked up her fourth consecutive victory in the women's race, a record which still stands.

Charlie Poulton, the San Antonio "fox," and Alex Kerr, Beverly Hills sporting goods dealer, came up with one of the truly great skeet exhibitions of all times at Indianapolis in 1942. These two machine-like performers hooked up in an amazing shoot-off. They each had broken 250 straight to tie for the All-Gauge Championship and the Texan needed another 175 straight to beat the curly-haired Californian.

Then there was that dramatic shoot-off between Herman Ehler of Dallas and Grant Ilseng, the Houston All-American, for the 1949 National High-Over-All crown at Dallas. They had tied with 544 of

550. Then Ehler broke a world record of 100 straight in the shoot-off to claim the victory.

Back in 1936 Dick Shaughnessy, 14-year-old boy wonder from Boston, won the National All-Gauge crown at St. Louis with 248 of 250, the youngest gunner ever to win this title. And Bobby Stack, then a 17-year-old Hollywood movie star, defeated the best men at the shoot when he captured the 20-gauge crown with 99 of 100. Then years later Francis Ellis, the greatest quail shot I ever hunted with, teamed up with Emmett Lee, a Jacksonville, Fla., detective, to win the 1950 National Two-Man championship with 499 of 500.

The professional gunners are outnumbered in skeet, but these great shots have staged some terrific battles for top honors in their own class. D. Lee Braun, who rates with Freddy Missildine of Sea Island, Ga., as the greatest pro skeet shots of all time, put on a show at the 1947 Syracuse Nationals that I will never forget.

Braun, a burly, six-foot-plus Texan, won the High-Over-All crown that year with 546 of 550, a world's record. He shattered 250 straight to win the all-gauge event and broke a pair of 100 straights to cop the 20-gauge and small gauge events, plus 96 of 100 to take the sub-small class. Missildine has furnished reporters with plenty of ink at the Nationals by winning the professional all-gauge event five times, twice with 250 straight.

One must also rate high the performance of a darkhorse, T.Sgt. Glenn W. Van Buren of Ft. Worth, Texas, a B-24 tail gunner who had been a prisoner of war in Germany. He won the National All-Gauge at Dallas with 249 of 250 and twice since has won the same title, both with 250 straight.

Ed Scherer, a photographer in Waukesha, Wis., made history with his shotgun in 1957 when he shot the highest average ever attained at either skeet or trapshooting. He combed the clays for a mark of .9970 on 1,200 targets.

Space doesn't permit the recounting of all the thrilling performances at skeet, but any list would be incomplete without mentioning the two-man show put on by Ed Calhoun and Johnny Dalton at the 1957 Nationals. These Maryland shooters won four National two-man team championships, another record that will stand for many a moon. Calhoun and Ben DiIorio, Los Angeles, were co-Captains of my 1958 All-America team. Last, but not least, was Chet Crites' (Detroit) thrilling victory in the 1954 Pan American at Caracas, Venezuela. Ken Pendergast, the Tallahassee All-American was victorious in the '56 Pan American at Mexico City. He scored 198 x 200.

Junior skeet shooters have done exceptionally well over the years, too. Aside from Dick Shaughnessy claiming the National All-Bore title when he was 14, Bobby Parker of Tulsa stunned the skeet world at San Francisco in 1949 when he captured the High-Over-All championship and the Junior title with 100 straight.

Another top junior in 1957 was 14-year-old Miner Cliett of Childersburg Ala., who won the 1957 Champion of Champions race with 100 straight over both men and women. Still another 100 straight was racked up by 12-year-old Eddie Brown of Birmingham, Mich., to win the sub-junior championship, a feat first accomplished by 13-year-old Eddie Harris of Galveston, Texas, in 1951.

Dick Shaughnessy of Boston won the National Allgauge Skeet Championship at St. Louis in 1936 when he was 14.

Movie actor Robert Stack (right) rests after winning the National 20-gauge skeet championship at St. Louis in 1936. Alex Kerr, (middle) has won more National Skeet championships than any gunner and actor Harry Fleischmann, also held All-American honors.

ALL-AMERICA SKEET CAPTAINS

1935—Henry B. Joy, Michigan

1936—Harry Fleishmann, California

1937—Frank Kelly, New Jersey

1938—Grant Ilseng, California

1939—Dick Shaughnessy, Massachusetts

1940—Dick Shaughnessy, Massachusetts

1941—Alex Kerr, California

1942—Dick Shaughnessy, Massachusetts

No skeet during war— 1943, 1944 and 1945

1946—D. Lee Braun, Texas

1947—Alex Kerr, California

1948—Grant Ilseng, Texas

1949—Grant Ilseng, Texas

1951—Alex Kerr, California

1952—Francis Ellis, Florida

1953—Louis Gordon, Arkansas

1954—John Dalton, Maryland

1955—Tom Mettler, California

1956—Alex Kerr, California

1957—Ed Calhoun, Maryland

1958—Ed Calhoun, Maryland, Co-Capt.

1958—Ben DiIorio, California, Co-Capt.

quail crazy

For all his fifty-five years, Knox O'Neal was built like an arrow, straight and thin, with the wit of a Hope and the eyes of a falcon. But he was quail crazy—plumb, unabashedly loco over bobwhites.

We hadn't traveled 500 yards along Tucker's grade before I found this out.

We—Art Smith and I—were guests of Pittsburgh lumber tycoon Fred Babcock on his vast and luxuriant Crescent B Ranch where he raises black Angus and Brahma cattle, near Punta Gorda, Florida. Knox O'Neal was his foreman and general manager for many years.

At the moment Knox was more absorbed in shepherding his old jeep along the winding sand tracks of Tucker's grade than he was in the ranch's several thousand cattle. We had gone scarcely 500 yards when a flock of turkey gobblers moved off the grade to let us pass.

My arm reached back for my shotgun and I saw Art's lips move in an unheard exclamation. Knox caught the action from the corner of his eye.

"No, Jimmy! Leave them gobblers for your city friends," he said. "We're after quail."

In fifty years of hunting everything that flies I had run into some interesting characters. But here was a new breed. "Leave 'em alone," he says, with a flock of gobblers not twenty yards from the jeep.

I thought of the fifteen pounds or so which one of those gobblers would add up to, and I knew it would take three quail to make up to one pound. Art, a Minnesota banker with a background of sixty years of hunting everywhere in America, was equally nonplussed.

"Jimmy!" Art turned toward me, his voice raspy with excitement. "I've never even seen a wild turkey before, let alone shoot one. And this quail-crazy guy makes me pass up my first chance. Oh, brother!"

I could sympathize with Art. We had been hunting quail with Dr. Walton Wall over at Orlando and had already seen enough to satisfy our gunning appetites. So we had driven over to meet Fred and his friends, which included Jack Dow and Jimmy Stewart from Minneapolis, Al Rockwell of Pittsburgh and Lloyd Dalzell from New York. All of them had hunted with me in Manitoba the fall before. Now Fred insisted we try his quail hunting.

As if to get our minds off the turkeys, Knox began chatting, more to himself than to us. "Used to manage Mr. Babcock's cattle ranches up in Georgia. But I ran my brains out chasing the critters from Georgia to Lake Okeechobee here in Florida. Bet I averaged more than 100,000 miles a year—and it interfered with my quail hunting. So I told Mr. Babcock he would have to hire another man for those outside jobs and I would take care of this ranch—where the quail are."

The morning was perfect for quail, soft and balmy, as we rattled along through patches of slash pine and long leaf pine, then into some tidewater cypress with swamp water on either side of the trail.

"Looka there!" Knox pointed ahead. A mother otter with several youngsters slid into the swamp. "Lots of wildlife in here."

We pulled out of the swamp onto higher ground again, but even here the heavy rains of the previous fall had left many depressions in the trail still under water. It reminded me of some of the old timber roads I had seen in Minnesota years before.

Still farther along a second flock of wild turkeys boomed off the road at our approach. Then a bunch of mallards hurtled upward from a puddle at the side of the trail. This was indeed a hunting paradise. I glanced at Art and noted he was getting fidgety. No one loved mallard shooting better than Art. But if Knox noticed my friend's plight he gave no sign. He just kept on driving and chatting.

"Them dogs we got in the crates in back," he said. "Trained 'em myself. Started 'em with a rubber ball until they got to retrieving good.

Then I finished 'em off on pine cones. That made 'em soft-mouthed and easy on quail."

A few minutes later we jumped two white-tail deer. They stopped a few yards off the trail and turned to watch us pass. They were tame as house dogs. This was beginning to turn into the most fantastic ride I had ever been on. Turkeys, otter, mallards and deer—all within a two-mile stretch of Tucker's grade. Just as we left the trail we jumped another flock of gobblers that disappeared into another cypress swamp.

By now I realized Knox wasn't kidding about loving quail. Art and I reconciled ourselves to settling for quail and nothing else. But Knox was chatting again.

"Before I went to work for Mr. Babcock I worked for the U. S. government's tick eradication program. Was hunting one day with my little .25-20 and I dropped a deer. Found it full of ticks. Discovered it was these deer that were the carriers of the Texas Fever tick and were spreading it through Florida's rangelands. So the government hired me to knock off all tick-infested deer so the disease wouldn't spread. Guess I must have shot 1,000 deer in five years. Got thirteen in one night."

When we finally arrived at a big, open patch of broom grass, studded with short palmettos, Knox stopped the jeep and let out the dogs. It was obvious he knew there were quail here, and so did the dogs.

"Wind's just right," he said, sniffing. "Got to watch that wind every minute so the dogs are always working into it."

I was reminded of my duck-hunting guides in Canada, to whom wind direction is everything. And I could agree that wind is just as important in quail hunting.

Knox's big pointer was ranging out in the palmettos. Suddenly he landed with all four brakes on and froze to a point. We tumbled out of the jeep and Art dived into his gear for his movie camera. Knox's eyes lit up like Halloween lanterns. I found myself understanding him better, for there is no thrill like the tension-packed thrill of walking in on a dog frozen in marble rigidity to a covey of quail.

We moved in rather fast, I thought, but then quail sometimes run instead of flushing. Art brought up in the rear, camera already grinding out footage of the scene. Then it happened.

What seemed like a dozen jet-propelled bundles of brown feathers catapulted up and outward like an expanding tornado. Two guns spoke,

Frances King, Atlanta, the only woman trapshooter to ever break 200 straight targets to win a state trapshooting title, is an enthusiastic quail hunter.

Harvey Blair, Kansas cattle rancher and oil tycoon, who loves quail hunting and pointers, tied for the Grand American Handicap trapshooting title in 1957.

catching the birds on the rise. At Knox's command the dogs searched out the four quail we had dropped and brought them in.

"Now we'll go after a few of the singles," said Knox. "They won't be far—just over there in the heavy cover."

With Art still working his camera we got three more singles. Then Knox indicated that would be enough out of this covey. These were all native quail, not planted stock, the true Florida bobwhite.

In a small growth of palmettos near the bank of a river we flushed another covey without getting a shot. "I'm afraid those birds headed to the water, but we can try to get up some singles," Knox said.

It was a perfect setting for a movie shot and Art got ready with the camera. The birds were in heavy bush cover next to the river and I had time to get in only one shot. Knox, too, got his shot off.

Art looked up, grinning. "I hope this sequence turns out good. Want to show it to the boys back in Minneapolis."

Knox and I looked at each other blankly. Even the nearest dog wore an expression of disappointment. Both Knox and I had missed cleanly. Art, his eye glued to the camera finder, hadn't noted that fact. But on the next covey he abandoned his camera for a gun and before noon the three guns had brought down thirty birds.

We had planned at breakfast that morning to meet at Babcock's wilderness cabin for lunch. Dalzell and Stewart were hunting with Robert McGee, one of Fred's riding foremen, and Babcock was guiding Jack Dow and Rockwell in another truck. Jack always sees to it that he hunts with the best shot, and perhaps in the back of his mind he knew that Fred Babcock would rate the best truck.

So at noon we pulled up to the cabin, surrounded by cypress on the bank of Jack Branch, a flowing swamp with water as clear as gin. It was an amazing structure. Fred had imported a man named Cozzette, the famous French-Canadian builder from Quebec, to cut cypress from the nearby wilderness and fashion it to the dimensions of the cabin.

Wild grapefruit and orange trees grew nearby, and the oranges we picked were as sweet as sugar. McGee explained the seeds for these wild trees had been dropped there by birds. Then he wanted to know if we cared to try a hand at fishing.

"You can catch bass up to eight pounds right from the porch," he said. "They never saw an artificial bait, either."

But we were more interested in the sights, particularly a 15-foot alligator that was sunning himself on a mud bank not far from the porch. It made me think of snakes. Knox had fitted us out with leather shin and calf guards when our hunt began. They were like the pads I used when I played hockey in Canada years before. But we hadn't seen a snake all morning.

"That's because our rattlers and moccasins are pretty dormant during the winter months," Fred explained. But he had a rule that a snake kit must be carried in each truck. "Just a sensible precaution," he added.

I remembered that in all the hunting I had done in Florida almost every winter since 1924 I had seen only two rattlesnakes. Knox admitted he'd lost only one dog from a rattlesnake bite in twenty-five years of hunting.

A few moments later McGee and Knox disappeared, saying they were going to cut down a palm tree and get us one of Babcock's delicious heart of palm salads for dinner. They trimmed the whole tree down to the base and cut out the heart at the bottom.

Then Gilbert Boddy, Fred's colored chef, went to work with an ear-to-ear grin that showed all of his teeth. He had brought along enough Brahma steer steaks to feed a threshing crew.

Right away Jimmy Stewart wanted to get into the act. He was an amateur chef back in Minneapolis, and, as we learned later, he is quite a cook. So he washed his hands, pulled up his sleeves and went to work with that ever-present grin on his face. Al Rockwell, who had just returned from Paris, immediately set out to try to tell Jimmy how to cook. Soon the tantalizing aroma of broiled steaks was wafted into us and Dalzell, hands in pockets, strolled in and announced in his Brooklyn brogue that dinner was ready.

"I've been used to those good old steaks that Chuck Saunders serves in Minneapolis," Jimmy Stewart commented later. "But now I've got to admit I've never eaten a better steak in my life than this one."

The heart of palm salad was equally good, with a rare, evasive flavor I'd never tasted before.

After dinner the talk turned naturally to quail, and Fred imparted some of the wonderful store of information he had on the bird.

"We've got two subspecies of quail here in Florida," he said. "In the north we have the eastern bobwhite and here in south Florida we

One of Fred Babcock's P

Junior All-America skeet shooter, Dickie Greco, Francis Ellis and Red Pitts
lunch with the dogs on Red's Florida ranch.

Art Stifal and Johnny Moran, two great shots, ready to sample Alabama's quail hunting.

have the Florida quail. Up north the 'bobs' will average about six ounces, but down south they average only five ounces. There's considerable overlap in the ranges where both subspecies intermix freely."

Then he told how Florida's population is growing so rapidly that the remaining wildlife land is being overrun with people, agriculture and other developments. He said as many as 1,000 families a week are moving into Florida, and this is cutting down what's left for quail. At the same time sale of hunting licenses has increased 85 per cent from 1946 through 1956.

Fred went on: "The problem that confronts our game men is this— land that used to support one quail per twenty acres will have to be managed so it'll support one quail per ten acres, because half of our quail land is being taken out of production."

Of course, on such an estate as Fred's Crescent B Ranch, with its vast acreage, the problem isn't as acute. And there quail thrive as they never could elsewhere. They thrive because there's plenty of food left out for them, such as acorns, wax myrtle, gallberries, cabbage palm fruits, slough grass, love vine and pine mast.

They also thrive because a lot of ideal nesting cover is left for mated pairs, such as broom grass, weedy fence rows and brushy areas where they can nest on the ground without too much molestation from man or predators. Coveys usually break up in early March and then the males do considerable mock battle with each other until a mate can be selected.

Once mated, the pair remains faithful until the coveys again assemble in the fall after the chicks are hatched. It takes the female from fifteen to twenty days to lay an average clutch of fourteen eggs. Then both she and the male take turns incubating the eggs. And if the female, for any reason, is killed, the male completes the incubation job alone.

By the 23rd day after incubation begins, the chicks start emerging from the shell. Under normal conditions 85 per cent of the eggs will hatch. Fifteen weeks later the young birds are fully grown and practically indistinguishable from the adults.

But the mortality, from the laid egg to a 15-weeks-old quail, is high. Some thirty-seven per cent of all nests are destroyed by natural enemies like skunks, cotton rats, snakes and ants. There is some re-nesting, but another twenty per cent are deserted due to disturbance by weather, man, livestock or other sources.

So the life of the quail is filled with danger from sources other than man. But perhaps this is just as well, because biologists claim a given amount of habitat will support only a certain number of birds. And more on that same land would only be wasted.

The biologists also claim that in Florida many coveys are never shot by hunters simply because they are never found. They figure hunters take only about thirty per cent of the quail population, but that eighty per cent disappears for one reason or another before the next hunting season. Fortunately, the quail themselves always seem to be able to replenish that eighty per cent loss under normal circumstances and in the better habitat. So in Florida, at least, rigid control of the harvest is admitted to be unnecessary and actually would be poor quail management.

"How about restocking quail?" Dalzell asked. Fred was ready with the answer.

"Game departments used to think it was the best way to get more birds," he said. "But that was mostly because the public demanded restocking. Then the game men found the return from restocking was negligible. They just weren't getting more birds.

"If you have quail on your land in the first place, the best way to get more is to plant the kind of cover they nest in and the kind of legumes and fruit-bearing shrubs they feed on. That's what we do here at Crescent B, and we have all the quail the land can support."

After this scholarly dissertation, we adjourned for the night. Next day I went hunting with Jack Dow, Fred and Bob McGee. Art Smith decided to spend the day taking movies and stills. Before we left, Fred picked up the modified bore 20-gauge I had used the day before, then the 12-gauge which Dalzell had used.

"What have you got there?" he asked. "Cannons? If you want to throw a lot of lead at those little birds, why don't you use 10-gauges?"

He walked over to the gun rack and brought down two little 28-gauges he kept there for his own quail shooting.

"Here, you two, take these today. They'll shoot straighter and you won't ruin your birds."

We didn't do much shooting, however, only enough to get a workout with the little 28s. It was more of a sight-seeing trip around the ranch. But when we routed out a wild hog in a bramble thicket, Fred spoke up.

"We'll let Jack Dow knock that critter off. It'll go pretty good for pork chops tonight."

Jack took the rifle that McGee handed him and with one shot put the porker down. Then the lithe cowboy dressed out the animal.

At dinner that night all of us pitched in with gusto on the delicious broiled chops. Later, letting a notch out of his belt, Stewart said, "I came down here to lose a few pounds. But how can I when you keep feeding me Brahma steer steaks, pork chops, heart of palm and quail?"

It was the climax of one of the greatest quail hunting trips of my life.

I'll never forget when I first made the acquaintance of Mr. Bob White. It was down on the Ray Loring farm near Marseilles, Ill., back in 1922 when I first started working for the American Trapshooting Association in Chicago. The first glimpse I ever got of these feathered puffballs bursting out of a patch of ragweed would have unhorsed me, if I'd been on a horse. That's how startling they are. The second covey, erupting in a tight bundle, made me think that here was a push-over target. Any blundering gunner should get five or six birds out of a spray like that.

I was wrong on two counts. Wrong to let myself get unnerved by the sight of so many birds flushing out of a tiny cover patch. And wrong to flock shoot them the second time. I soon found out they are a much more explosive target, and a much smaller one, than our Manitoba prairie chicken, which I had hunted since I was knee high to a beagle. You just don't flock shoot quail. There's more air than you think between them. You pick your bird and you try to bring that one bird down. When I learned this I began to get real enjoyment out of quail hunting. I still rank Mr. Bob the number one target for any gun, and the greatest table delicacy of them all.

That's saying quite a lot, because it didn't take me long to find out that Mrs. Loring had no peer in the fried chicken and country bacon departments, two gastronomical areas in which I was a loving devotee.

After the trapshooters moved their head office to Vandalia, Ohio,

I had to be satisfied with cottontails and the odd pheasant, so far as hunting was concerned. Sure, Vandalia had quail—just behind the gun club—but they were on the song bird list. For that I never could quite forgive the game commissioners.

During the early years at Vandalia, Charlie "Sparrow" Young used to come over to the gun club and coax me away for a hunt in the old Ohio quail haunts. Charlie, who lived in Springfield, Ohio, was one of the world's greatest live pigeon shots. He also was deadly on game and a terrific trapshooter. I'm sure he attended every Grand American from 1900 until he passed away a few years ago.

In those early days live pigeons were used at many shoots instead of clay targets, and some of the shoots were conducted on live sparrows. Charlie won so many of these pigeon and sparrow shoots his pals got to calling him "Sparrow" Young. The name stuck until he died. He was the first trapshooter to break 100 straight from twenty-three yards to win the Grand American. And that was in 1926 when he was seventy years old.

Well, as I said, Charlie loved quail hunting, and I guess because he loved it so he didn't agree with the game department that quail should be on the song bird list in Ohio. Eventually his arguments convinced me, too. One day Sparrow and I were hunting around Celina when I flushed a covey of "bob whites." My trigger finger was so itchy that before I knew it I had downed a couple fluff tufts. Then I didn't know what to do with them, because it was opening day of the rabbit season and the woods were crawling with game wardens.

So I shouted over to Sparrow, "I got a hole in my shooting jacket. Can you carry these birds for me?"

He took them with considerable relish, fancying the fine supper he'd have that night. Ten minutes later we were stopped by a pair of law men. My heart sank and I couldn't get a word out. But Charlie was a sly one. The wardens had seen him breaking clays at the gun club and they started talking about trapshooting. They never inquired about our hunting luck. That saved our hides, but you can bet it was the last quail shooting I did in Ohio.

A few years later I began to probe into Arkansas for quail hunting and had some wonderful shoots with Bill Dickey, then catching for the New York Yankees, and his brother "Skeets," who caught for the Chicago White Sox. The Dickey boys lived in Little Rock, still do for

In Texas and Mexico they boast that Ulan Hill never misses. He has one straight run of 87 quail.

When I snapped this picture, Bill Dickey, was the great New York Yankee catcher. Bill still hunts quail six days a week during the season.

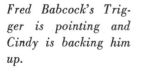

Fred Babcock's Trigger is pointing and Cindy is backing him up.

that matter, and were widely known as the best Bob White hunters in the Razorback state.

Bill and Skeets hunted six days a week, had a fine string of pointers and both were crack shots. Each was well over six feet tall, so when they came to a fence they would merely step over it and then Bill would hold up the wire so I could roll under. He knew every farmer in the state, or so it seemed, and he always carried a few autographed baseballs for the farm kids. This was cheaper than laying out a $100 bill for the hunting rights on the best farms. Of course, every wise hunter makes it a practice to take care of the farmer, either with a present for his wife, some shells for him, candy for the kids, or by sharing the game. But the Dickeys were the only two guys I ever knew who traded Yankee baseballs for the choicest quail hunting in Arkansas.

Eventually I worked my way up the quail shooter's ladder until I got an invitation to hunt on the famous King ranch in Texas. On the 920,000 acres of this vast ranch is some of the finest quail shooting in the world.

One year I hunted quail there with Jack Dempsey, and I must confess I never had any better shooting. Jack went overboard for the wild turkey hunting because, he said, "They're easier to hit." That might be so, but on the King ranch you shot them in the head with a rifle and that just wasn't for me. So while Jack concentrated on turkeys, I specialized on the Bob Whites and Clara, the better half, spent most of her time browsing around the barn admiring the Kleberg horses and cattle.

Dick Kleberg and his son Dick, Jr., ran the ranch while Bob Kleberg took charge of the racing stables, one of the largest and best in the world. They even had a half-mile track back of the barn for workouts and I still have pictures of Clara riding Bold Venture and Assault on exercise runs. Both are former Kentucky Derby winners.

Dick Kleberg, who passed away a few years ago, was one of the greatest hunters I ever knew. He was a crack shot both with a rifle and shotgun and he had a nose like a bird dog. Bob was more interested in fast horses as a hobby. The King Ranch still is one of the finest wintering grounds for ducks and geese in America.

I'm sure there were at least fifty bird dogs in the Kleberg kennels and each morning Dick would say, "I'm giving you my five best dogs.

198

Go out and get us a mess of Bob Whites." Then he'd assign a guide and a station wagon for the day and off I'd go. Often we'd raise twenty coveys of quail in a single morning.

I also had the pleasure of riding in Dick's favorite hunting wagon, built for him by his friends Harlow Curtice, now General Motors board chairman, and Harley Earle, designer for Cadillac.

Aside from the King ranch, some of the greatest quail shooting in the world lies in Mexico. Ulan Hill, a top-cut hunter from the Lone Star state, will vouch for that. I've seen covies of more than a hundred Bob Whites in Mexico. And when I compared such spectacles with quail hunting in Minnesota, my native state, it made me a little sick. Mr. Bob White has just about had it in the Gopher state.

The winters are too severe; proper cover and feed is lacking, and the Bob White has disappeared from all but four or five counties in Southeastern Minnesota where remnant covies still exist. But 20-plus years ago I enjoyed some fine quail hunting around Hutchinson, Minnesota, with Jeff Jones, then co-owner of the old Minneapolis Journal, and Frank Boyle, the game warden.

But quail are plentiful in Cuba and I've taken more than one limit within a stone's throw of Havana with Frankie Steinhart, the Cuban railway magnate. I also have walked my legs off with old Cap Hardy, the one-time famous rifle and pistol shooter, in California. But I never cared much for California quail because they always ran much faster than I could. And in Alabama, where I hunt wild turkeys, I have made an occasional foray for quail when I got tired of sitting on a log calling gobblers. But I must admit, Alabama quail shooting was pretty spotty, at least where I hunted.

Florida, however, is something else again—call it quail heaven. I can still remember the winter Vandalia, or Baby Grand American trapshoot staged at Eustis, Florida, back in 1924. Those were the days when you could bag a basketful of Bob Whites in a ten-minute ride out of Eustis.

In those days I hunted with the Miller boys from Eustis, and they owned the best three braces of bird dogs I had seen in years of roaming quail country. They also owned the hardware store at Eustis and ran a gun club on the side. So that year of the Baby Grand I spent a month with them hunting quail and fishing bass.

199

When the boys were too busy in the store, they would turn their dogs over to me. Then I'd pick up Moon Baker, a colored boy, at the edge of town. He was an orange picker by trade, but his first, last and always love was hunting quail. He charged me fifty cents a day as a guide fee, but I furnished the refreshments and, if necessary, the lunch.

Now Moon was deathly afraid of rattlesnakes. He always wore high shin pads to guard against their strikes. One of his constant concerns was the fact that I refused to wear shin pads and seemed content in my Red Wing bird hunter boots.

One day Moon went wandering off to look for a dog that had turned up missing. Presently I heard the loudest scream I had ever heard in my life, not even barring the trenches of France in World War I. It was Moon. He came running.

"Mistah Jimmy." He paused for a breath. "I nearly stepped on the biggest rattler in Florida."

"Where?" I asked. Moon pointed, speechless now. I walked to the spot and there was a six-foot rattler still coiled and ready to strike. A dose of No. 9 chilled stretched him out.

In Florida rattlers are semi-dormant in winter months and you seldom see them while hunting. In fact, I have seen only two rattlesnakes in all my Florida quail hunting. But this was the one that made the exception to the rule. So, for anyone contemplating a Florida quail hunt, I would suggest leather leggings, or knee-high boots, and even then it would be prudent to have a snake bite kit with you.

Once the Sarasota Chamber of Commerce lined up a quail hunt for me on the old Colonel Jake Ruppert cattle ranch near Ft. Meyers. Ruppert was the owner of the New York Yankees. I had met him at the French Lick, Indiana, skeet shoot where he told me about the fabulous quail shooting on his ranch. When I got there I looked around for the dogs and saw none. Instead the guide came out with a low-pocket mongrel that looked like a beagle hound whose dam had been disappointed in life.

"That's the best quail dog in America," the guide confided.

It was too late to turn back, so I accepted the statement with private reservations. We started hunting in the palmettos and the guide let the dog run. When he came back barking my quail expert said, "Now follow me; he's got 'em spotted." Sure enough, the birds were where the dog said they would be. Before I realized it, we had our limit.

"Say," the guide blurted. "Do you know any of those big league ball players around Sarasota?"

I admitted I knew a few.

"Well, I had just as good a quail dog as this here Mike we're hunting with," the guide said. "But those baseball buggers borrowed my dog and never did bring it back."

Later I learned that Paul Derringer, ace pitcher for the Cincinnati Reds, had borrowed my guide's dog. But it had run away and Paul was afraid to confess the fact.

One of the really great quail hunters in Florida is Dr. Walton Wall, the Orlando trapshooting champ. It was he who won the Washington 1,000-target meet the past two years straight, as well as the Fourth of July championship at Miami last year. Doc has a perfect quail dog, a seven-year-old pointer that knows more about quail than they do.

And Doc himself is in the right profession for quail hunting. He's an eye doctor, and he has the eye of a hawk, which you need for quail hunting. More than that, he's lightning fast with a scattergun, as Ted Culbertson and Art Smith can verify after one of our Florida quail hunts. It was only through Dr. Wall's charity that we were permitted to get any shooting at all.

I've spent some fine afternoons with Dr. Walton Wall and Charlie Arnold, his hunting partner. The doctor's favorite pointer is "Sir Mike," and I am told that more than 5,000 Bob Whites have been shot over this great dog. During the quail season Doc hunts four afternoons a week, rain or shine. He has a Willis jeep with a box behind for his dogs. There's a seat atop the box for one of the party to keep tabs on the canine corps while the doctor drives. Then, when likely cover is reached, three dogs are loosed to work game with two staying in the kennel box for relief.

Few coveys are missed, but the doctor is a conservationist as well as a hunter. He won't permit more than five or six birds to be shot out of a covey. Then he bruskly directs, "That's all. We've had enough out of this covey. Let's get on to another." He believes, rightly, in leaving seed to preserve this fine sport.

Now, I have been called a good duck shot. But the fact is that I have been outshot by a good many people—women, children and the aged. For example, Max Fleischmann, a major in the first World War, was 74 years old when I went hunting with him on the Hope Plantation in South Carolina in December, 1950. And I'll never forget my first impression of him—a short, bushy-eyebrowed, white-haired bundle of energy. His years as a lightweight boxer and semi-pro baseball player showed in every wirey movement he made.

Clara and I had been invited to his Hope Plantation fifty miles out of Charleston, S. C., to hunt duck and quail. The plantation was his private hunting lodge embracing nearly 8,000 acres on the edge of a huge cypress swamp. The typical southern mansion that graced the plantation was flanked by oak trees decked in Spanish moss, cornfields and dog kennels. Half a mile away was duck slough that you dream about. A large staff of Negro servants kept appearing at odd moments to answer your slightest wish in food and drink.

Quail hunters, Charlie Arnold and Dr. Walton Wall. Dr. Wall, Orlando, Florida eye surgeon, and trapshooter, is known locally as Mr. Quail.

Photo by Jimmy Robinson

I'll never forget this snow-thatched master literally bounding up a winding staircase to fetch a photograph of one of his better quail hunts so we could enjoy it with him. Nor will I forget the Currier and Ives hunting prints that adorned the walls of that staircase. And then he would talk about his dogs, the best I had seen excepting the King ranch pack.

Then, on the next morning we went out, through the lonely picked cornfields, past brush-lined ditches and alder thickets along the creeks. And Max Fleischmann, to whom hunting was a passion, turned to me and said, "Jimmy, you have a goose cannon. Here, take one of my .410s. We're after quail."

Now every experienced goose hunter knows that a man who is proficient on quail and accustomed to a small-bore shotgun can make

I snapped this picture of the late Major Max Fleischmann while hunting with him at his Hope Plantation in South Carolina. Of all the sportsmen I have ever known, the Major was tops.

The dog I used on Colonel Jake Ruppert's ranch in Florida was a cross between a beagle and an unknown, but proved to be one of the best quail dogs I have ever hunted over.

Photo by M. J. Bell, Sr.

a sucker out of the greatest goose shot that ever lived. That is, he can until he tries goose shooting. Then he'll soon find out that he wants all the gun he can get. The techniques are entirely different.

But here I was, a goose shooter, about to be offered up on the altar of quail hunting ritual. Max Fleischmann was taking advantage of me and, judging by his chuckles, it was making him very happy. He was shooting a .410 double.

The first covey we raised I missed completely with the borrowed .410. Out of the next two coveys Max dropped ten quail with twelve shots and he was very happy. Even cocky.

Now it happened that Max was carrying two boxes of cigars along to provide for the dull moments between coveys. One box was a cedar affair containing dollar cigars hand-made in Cuba. The other was a box of 10-cent cigars. I had seen him offer a guest a dollar cigar after dinner, but give the victim a 10-cent cigar to fill his pockets for the hunt.

Somehow, on that first morning of our quail hunt, I made a slight mistake. I got my fingers in Max's box of dollar cigars before we started on the hunt and filled my pockets with them. To make up the loss I filled the first layer of the dollar box with 10-cent cigars.

Every time the Major would knock down a double on quail he would turn to me and chuckle. And I, with a dollar cigar in my puss, would smile back. After the shoot was over the head dog trainer whispered to me:

"The Major outshot you today, Jimmy, but you sure outsmoked him."

It was a highlight of my many years of acquaintance with Max Fleischmann. When I first met him over thirty years ago he was an avid live pigeon shooter at Kentucky shoots. At one time he owned a million-dollar fishing boat, but found hunting in Africa more to his liking. When Teddy Roosevelt, his good friend, wanted to go to Africa, he came to Max first to find out all about it. In his last years the old gentleman developed a keen interest in Ducks Unlimited and became one of its greatest supporters.

There wasn't a top fishing stream or a lake in the world that he had not fished. But hunting was his first love, and of all the quarry he hunted, quail topped it all in the Fleischmann book.

CHAPTER THIRTEEN

ROCKETS
of the NORTH

Into this rocket-minded world the speedy bluebill fits most admirably. If there is jet propulsion among birds it all started with him. As he rides the northern gales he comes with the speed of a bullet, and he is gone before the slow-minded hunter can get his gun to his shoulder.

For those who love duck hunting the time of the bluebill is the high mark of the year.

Few birds are speedier, few offer a more sporting target. And, above all, few are more obliging in responding to decoys. For the bluebill, scaups to the hunters on the eastern shore, is a gregarious little bundle of energy. He loves company and he will arrow into your stool with the greatest of confidence, even eagerness. Another high recommendation for him is his edibility. There are fewer tastier birds than these Delta marsh jets.

As the great Delta marsh at the southern shores of Lake Manitoba begin to freeze for the winter, a great wave of bluebills comes hurtling down from the north. They pile in. They bore in. They zoom over. They are like bullets. They are like slugs from a multimachine-gun nest singing over your head. The air in the more concentrated migrations of gray and blackish dots is darkened like a blackbird invasion.

207

The French-Canadian natives of the Delta region, who trace back their ancestry to the long-gone days of the fur voyageurs, and know well all the prairie ducks from long and close association, wait impatiently for this bluebill flight. Yes, the canvasback is a fine duck, they say, and the mallard, and others. But they'll take the little bluebill. They always have. Barring a local dropping of an atomic bomb, they probably always will.

Picturesque and apt of speech, especially in English, which for them remains a second tongue, the Delta French Canadians have a word for bluebills. They call them "nordern" bluebills. Not bluebills. Never. They are always "nordern" bluebills. And that is as fine a tribute —remember, it is a totally subconscious one—as I could write to the little bluebill in a thousand times as many words.

For the real north is a place of superlatives to the Delta natives, as it is, in a sense, to all of us who live in more clement climes. It stretches there before them, vast, primal, elemental, to the Arctic Sea. It is "down north" to them, and it rifles down the savage arctic gales, the fierce prairie blizzards. They know, and many of their ancestors helped to make, its glorious traditions. From the north come the great local flights of waterfowl, the big Canada geese, the outsize mallard drakes with the curl in their tails, the heavy canvasbacks, and others. And from there come these spectacular bluebill flights, racing the arctic gales that bring the final freeze-up, providing, as they have for centuries, a portion of the natives' winter's provender.

The beloved, inevitable "nordern" is not a plagiarized Scandinavian accent, lifted bodily from the Swede settlers scattered thereabouts. It is completely indigenous. The "nord," or *nor'*, is the French for English north, which the Delta people have never recognized, or rather, pronounced. The apt English adjectival ending has been adopted, but with small concession to the unfamiliar and difficult digraph "th."

The Manitoba Delta Marsh is one of the great waterfowl breeding and resting places of the continent. Some sixty miles west of Winnipeg, it is a vast expanse of marsh cane, bulrush and cattail islands in a sea of shallow, food-rich water. Twenty miles long and several miles wide, it attracts most of the waterfowl species of the continental interior, both as breeders and as migrators. In the spring, as soon as the first slivers of open water appear along the island borders, the first ducks make their appearance (not the bluebills). In the fall, the marsh is

208

frozen tight and hard before the last ducks leave. The great bulk of the tag-end migrants are the little bluebills. When the last open water in the marsh glazes over, there always are die-hard bluebills that raft up in great Manitoba Lake.

The "nordern" bluebill exodus at the freeze-up always is the most spectacular duck flight of the year. One day the weather turns, and suddenly the chilling bite of deep winter is in the air. A film of ice creeps out over the marsh. The open water contracts steadily. The teeming bluebills on the marsh, a good percentage of which rode down the last lusty north wind, are nervous, restless, as a disturbing, age-old instinct stirs within them. Presently, the restlessness may take on the look of approaching panic. The birds seems in a quandary of indecision. They fly up quickly in little bunches, settle down in another part of the marsh, only to find that is not to their liking, and they are on the wing again, and again they settle down. The bunches get larger and larger. Phone calls to Tom Nelson at Fergus Falls—to Dick Bonnycastle at Winnipeg—to Ed Chesley at Petersfield in Manitoba—would reveal that a brisk northwest wind had sprung up, more likely than not an incipient blizzard. In the afternoon the northwest blow has reached the marsh. A few bluebills ride before it. Just before twilight a flock of marsh "bills" rise into the wind. Others join them. They swing around over the marsh in a great majestic circle until they feel the wind's hard push behind them. Then they straighten out and head southeast, pin-pointed for their next stop and their wintering grounds. Big flock after big flock takes off after them.

Now great flights of birds from the north begin to come over the marsh, sometimes when weather abnormally compresses the flight, in tier on tier, reaching high, high in the air. When light fails the sky is full of ducks, most of them "nordern" bluebills, as far to the north and the west, and the east, and the south, and as high, as the eye can see. Far into the night the birds can be heard—brrrr, brrrr, brrrr— passing overhead, the purring murmur of tens of thousands of "bills" blended by the distance, sounding like a distant roaring waterfall.

In the morning, if the storm has been a bad one, most of the great flocks have gone from the marsh. Practically, the season's shooting is over. If any open water remains, these patches will have their bluebills. Out on the great lake, bluebills will still be rafted. If the storm petered out during the night, the open water oasis of the marsh, and especially the lake, may still hold great numbers of die-hard bluebills, northern birds which swooped in during the night. But even these will be an anticlimax.

This is the time the typical bluebill hunter, who can sit in a freezing blind, battered by the elements, and not only live through it but like it, lives for the rest of the year. In the cities and small towns to the south, as the duck season draws to its close, these counterparts of the Delta natives have restlessly marked time, impatiently scanning the weather reports, waiting for news of the beginning of this flight. When it comes, there is an exodus to the shooting lodges similar to that of opening day. The "nordern" bluebill flight over its main route is the most dependable of all the species.

For the little bluebill, more than any other interior species as a whole, flies by the weather. An experienced, observant gunner to the south by keeping tab on the weather to the north, can forecast pretty closely when the bluebills will come piling over his favorite sloughs and passes, usually eager to be lured down to a rest and feed by inviting stools. Out of the north sweep the the bullet flights, often in single file like great black pencil lines against the sky. Riding their favorite blasting wind, they may be zooming at sixty or seventy or even more, miles an hour. Then there is pass shooting at its very best. Or, scudding before the wind, they may suddenly shoot into the decoys. Normally, perhaps, most flights will arrive at night. Then, still nervous, erratic, jumpy, moving in short, quick flights about the marsh, the bluebill will provide some memorable shooting in the morning.

This medium-sized, handsome, black and white duck (the drake) is the swashbuckler of the airways. He's the hot fighter pilot of the duck family. He's the aerial acrobat, the daring young drake on the flying trapeze. Riding the high north wind across a pass, he laughs at all but the most instinctive shooters. The sky may be empty, the next moment he is overhead. In high, rough weather, which he loves, he likes to hedgehop. He comes from nowhere. The good bluebill shooter at these times has to be on his toes. He would be much happier if he had eyes like a fly—everywhere. Apparently drunk as a lord on the wine of the north wind and the mysterious call of the season, the bluebills may come in from all sides, at all levels, now skimming over the surface of the water, now swooping down from above. Stand up sud-

210

denly in your blind or your boat and you're likely to get your cap knocked off—if not your head.

I was hunting once with Clair Lantz at the Delta, and it was that kind of a day. We were in a boat in some scant rushes. The bluebills were zooming over before the wind like bullets. Clair saw a few coming and stood up to make them flare. He was a little slow. The lead bird, sizzling up so fast that Lantz afterward swore he saw him smoke, smacked him on the head. Clair sailed overboard in a flat curve like he had been hit by a 75mm shell. He cleaved the water neatly with his head, about ten feet away, but unfortunately his spread-eagled legs and arms, not to mention the gun, detracted from the effect of his dive considerably.

Clair had a little trouble extricating his head from the marsh bottom and I was about to go in after him when he stood up groggily in about four feet of water, pond weeds draped like a milliner's latest exclusive model about his noggin. He was occupied for a while clearing mud out of his nose and mouth and eyes, and sputtering for breath. Then he muttered, "Why didn't you tell me we were shooting jet fighters this morning?"

Another time I was with Emil Lamirande, ace French-Canadian guide, on a narrow point extending into the Delta marsh, and the bills had again been drinking deep in the north wind and the season. I put Jules Emma and Dinty Moore on Jimmy's pass, between the big lake and Cadham's bay, and I was on a point extended across a flyway, 200 yards away, and the birds, riding a gale, were passing it hell-bent, like black and white and brown meteors, virtually just above the shore growth. Emil and I were crouched in it. It limited our lateral field of vision. Lamirande's job was to watch for incoming ducks and give me the signal when to jump up for a shot. Then the birds would flare and my pump would speak. That was the theory. The trouble was, it wasn't working. Emil would give his signal, I would bounce up like a spring-steel jumping jack. And I would have my gun practically knocked out of my hands by feathered projectiles that shot past so fast the swish of their wings and bodies reminded me of an express train. Several flocks went by in this manner, with no more damage than a momentary fright occasioned by an apparition that suddenly sprang out of the ground into their midst and then as suddenly subsided again.

They couldn't hear me barking at Emil after I hit the dirt when the last flight passed.

"For Pete's sake," I pleaded with Emil, "can't you give me a decent lead on those berserk bluebills?"

Emil shook his head humbly. "In twenty years, Jimmy," he said, "I never seen anything like this. I look up, but this blessed grass, I cannot see. It wave like mad, it bothers me. Before I see, dere dey are. I do my best."

Emil maneuvered to where he could catch the birds a little sooner. He lengthened his "lead." Now he gave his signal when the oncoming "bills" were still at least sixty yards out. I would pop up as though I had suddenly sat down hard on a tack. We finally got the thing co-ordinated so I had those boiling birds flaring at about forty yards, and I was able to pick out my "bills" at a decent shooting distance. Those sizzling bluebills that day gave me some shooting I will long remember.

I saw my first little "nordern" bluebills on the Delta marsh in 1903, a good many years before I would be eligible to discard my short britches. I didn't know a bluebill from a whooping crane. My Grandfather Cruikshank, who lived in Winnipeg at that time and loved duck shooting as well as he loved his race horses, which was a great deal, took me with him on a hunting trip to the marsh. I was too young to shoot, but my love for duck shooting dates from that time. It has been a rare year since when I haven't returned—some say like a bad penny—to the Delta marsh in the fall for a duck hunt. And every year I have never failed to treat myself to at least one real shoot on those late-flying torpedoes, the "nordern" bluebills. Of course, the flights, as those of other ducks, are not what they used to be. I do not want to give the impression that bluebills have not suffered from the same causes that have decimated other species, because emphatically they have. With the necessary modern limits, the old-time bluebill shoots are a thing of the past. But the little bluebill, ornery, erratic, complacent, persistent little devil that he is, will probably be with us as long as any duck. Let us hope that will be forever.

I killed my first duck in 1906 at Dead Lake, in Minnesota, near Richville, in the northwest, where my mother had moved that year from Winnipeg. It was a bluebill. I killed it with a $4.95 single barrel, my first gun, which I bought with the first money I earned myself—selling the Chicago Blade & Ledger, besides which its notorious descendants of the Roaring Twenties were rather staid and decorous family journals, at the Richville sawmill. I was hunting with Clayt Peterson and his brothers, all a little older than I, on their farm off Dead Lake. I still hunt with Clayt in the same spot to this day.

In the next several years, bluebills kept me out on the marshes and lakes around Richville. It was, and is, one of the great duck regions of the country. Besides the famous Dead Lake, there were Marion, Pine, Star, Walker, Pickerel, all still fine duck producers, and many others. A boat was easy to borrow from a friendly farmer. "Store" decoys we had never seen. We used what we called "blocks," which we made from chunks of half-rotted wood. A length of twine and a stone made a decoy anchor. We anchored these half-baked decoys in front of a rude blind, and they did the trick, particularly with the bluebills, which in late season always were the most numerous ducks.

There is a lot to be said for our old way of hunting. Naturally, it will never come back. There always were plenty of ducks, and plenty of places to shoot. About our only worry was shells, and we loaded these ourselves. There were no city hunters in those days, and the farmers, with the tractor and the combine still over the horizon, were all too busy to shoot. The roads during the autumns would have been impassable to automobiles, but so far as I know there was only one gas buggy in the county, and it wasn't ours. Gumbo mud, though, was no barrier to our youthful shanks. On a red-letter day we were able to borrow a buggy from Granddad Robinson, a lumber man in these parts.

My youthful duck bags were usually heaviest with bluebills. No day was too cold or blustery if a bluebill flight was on. If a good flight happened to coincide with a school day, my intake of formal knowledge would be apt to undergo a hiatus on that day. Numerous were the lickings for which the bluebills were responsible. I was singularly unsuccessful in my efforts to impress the proper authorities with the soundness of my conception of the relative importance of the bluebills and school.

Bluebills coming down with a hard wind provide just about the sportiest shooting you will find. I had several good bluebill shoots one fall, but the sportiest came, strangely enough, the day after the

The late Fred Miller of Milwaukee found out that bluebills were jet-propelled.
Fred was Notre Dame football Captain in 1927 and an All-American.

Photo by Bruce Reinecker

Emil gave me the signal when the "bills" were sixty yards from the blind.

Photo by Al Ridinger

Delta marsh began to freeze tight. It was due solely to herculean ice-breaking efforts on the part of the late Freddie Miller of Milwaukee, the Notre Dame football all-American of some years back.

Freddy flew up late on October 22, with Walt Taylor, Pat McClain, Mike Droney, and Chuck Murphy. I had been telling him about the tag-end bluebill, and bull canvasback, shooting on the marsh for years. Now here he was at last, and the marsh was freezing up. In addition, snow had started to fall. Only that afternoon, my wife, Clara, who is the major-domo of the camp, had been insisting it was time to close up our Sports Afield lodge. The shooting season, so far as the weather was concerned, was over. I was in a quandary. There still would be plenty of bluebills left in the morning—barring an old-fashioned blizzard—both on the big lake and on any open water remaining in the marsh. I wanted Fred to get the "nordern" bluebill and can shooting (assuming any cans remained) he had set his heart on. But the only place to get it was well out in the marsh. And the marsh was freezing over.

I took Fred to one side and tried to explain the situation.

"With this near-zero weather and no wind," I said, "the marsh is going to be frozen tight in the morning. We can't get out there. I'm afraid you'll have to forget the bluebills and the cans. But how about a stubble shoot on big northern mallards? They've been working over Bill McCowan's field over there the last few days."

I went to the window and pointed. The barley field was half a mile away, but we could see the mallards swarming over it. Freddie nodded. Sure. It was O.K. But I could see the deep disappointment in his eyes.

After supper that evening we sat around the lodge. Another season was coming to an end. Walt Taylor and Chuck (Rip Van Winkle) Murphy, who had shot in the barley stubble that afternoon, described their field shoot in glowing terms. Young Mike and Henry Mulder, who also had arrived that afternoon, could not wait to get out to the field in the morning. I looked at Freddie Miller. He was listening attentively, but it was plain it was not mallards he wanted on the morrow; he wanted die-hard bluebills drunk with the north wind, bluebills riding on a gale, scudding over a pass, such as I had described to him.

Mike Droney, a reincarnated Baron von Manchausen with a bottomless fund of tall duck stories, had been dozing by the fire. Now, refreshed, he ambushed the conversation. He took us down to Iowa of the early 20's, and sketched a graphic picture of long-gone days, of mammoth duck migrations that would never be again, and shoots that could never again be duplicated. A spell of nostalgia gripped me and I forgot about Freddie Miller.

At length Rip Murphy, the old blind-snoozer, roused, looked around and asked, "Where is Fred?"

"All he's talked about for a month is late bluebills and cans," observed Irvin O'Connor, who had made the air trip to the camp with Miller and Joe Laird, the pilot. "He's probably snooping around the marsh."

I slipped outside, and a buzz of talk, mostly excited French, led me to the guide shack. There was Mr. Miller, trying hard to slip a calm Anglo-Saxon word edgewise now and then into a spate of Gallic-English from Frank and Ed Lavelle, two of our French-Canadian guides.

"The boys tell me, I think, they can break through the ice and we can get a bluebill shoot in the morning," Fred greeted me with an apologetic grin. The Lavalle boys nodded vigorously.

I was dubious. I argued the new ice would be pretty solid by morning, that it was a job for an icebreaker to get through the mile or so to the island that we would have to reach to get across the flyway —the path the birds would use between the lake and what would proba-bly be the only open water remaining in the marsh, Cadham's Bay. But I consented to make the try. I dragged Fred away from the guides, who would have jabbered "nordern" bluebills all night, and we went to bed.

Five minutes later (it seemed) Big George Rennie, former Moun-tie, our chief cook, who never can get it through his skull he can't beat me at gin rummy, had me by the legs and was dragging me out of my bunk, in a last-ditch effort to awaken me. I almost froze before I got into my clothes. The lodge shivered in a virtual gale from the northwest. I went into the dining room to cross to Freddie's room to awaken him, and found him halfway through his breakfast of Rennie Special Canadian bacon and wheat cakes.

Ed and Frank, the two Lavalle boys, came in and we went down to the marsh shore. Freddie greeted the wind with a glad eye. As far as

Baron Hilton of hotel fame and Mrs. Jimmy Robinson looking over a bag of Lake Manitoba bluebills.

Photo by Art Rogers, Eau Claire, Wisconsin

Artist Roger Preuss bagged these northerns at Dead Lake in Minnesota where I killed my first duck in 1906. He painted the 1949 federal duck stamp.

Photo by Jimmy Peterson,
Minneapolis Tribune

we could see, to the island and beyond, the marsh was frozen. I walked out a little way on the shore ice, and it seemed as solid as concrete.

"Freddie, Ed and Frank," I said, "you have your work cut out for you. If you think you can break that ice all the way out to the island, you're welcome to try. But kindly include me out!"

Freddie, an assistant football coach at Notre Dame, who frequently scrimmaged with the boys, was not daunted. "Come along, Ed," he said. Grabbing a heavy handmade oar which was like a war club, he pushed a boat on the ice and began belaboring it. Slowly he and Ed opened a channel. Frank and I followed in the other boat.

Dawn broke, gray and overcast. The wind howled. The cold was bitter. I worked up a mild sweat, however, just watching the herculean labors of Fred and Ed. Bluebills scooted past to the west, headed for Cadham's Bay. In order to look busy, I picked up my gun and assiduously did some dry shooting, which, as any honest hunter knows, is a back-breaking, man-killing exercise. Occasionally Fred would seize a second or two from his labors to contemplate the darting bluebills. He reminded me of a famished far-north explorer sighting, at long last, a herd of meaty caribou. Then he would return to his beloved toil with quadrupled vigor.

Yard by yard the stubborn channel lengthened. I was bundled up like an Eskimo infant, but the wind was driving the cold into my bones. Freddie and Ed had long since removed their outer coats.

It was two hours before we reached the island. The bluebills were still scooting by, trading between the lake and the bay. Stamping my feet, which were like ice blocks, I stationed Freddie on the island's south shore, in bulrushes, and I took a place seventy-five yards away. We shoved our cork and balsa decoys out on the ice in front of us. The wind was now terrific, an occasional gust practically lifting us off our feet. It was coming from an angle, behind us.

The bluebills—and a few late bull cans—coming from the lake were skidding before it. Now and then a mighty gust would catch them and they would hurtle by like miniature rockets. We would pick up a flock in the distance, small and black, boring toward us. Quickly they grew larger. Then in a moment they were over us and past. Fred's double would blast. My pump might blast, or it might not. To my surprise, I was hopelessly slow on these rocketing birds. My heavy clothes were catching my gun butt.

There was a lull in the flight, and I noticed that the wind had dropped. Then it began blowing again, from the opposite direction. Birds were in the air again. The wind picked up soon, it seemed, and was blasting by with even more ferocity than a short time before from the other way. I started to shed my coat, but decided against it. It was too cold. A few bluebills torpedoed by. I had just four ducks down when Fred's Labrador picked up his tenth duck, his limit. Fred came over, crouching in the wind, with his ducks, eight "bills" and two bull cans, and asked me what I thought of the shooting.

"Some character must have put baking powder in my shells," I grunted. "Duck down, here comes a flight!"

A flock of "bills" was riding a hurricane gust, highballing up at an incredible velocity. One moment they were half a mile off, the next they were hurtling by overhead, off to the side. I led the lead bird instinctively and let fly. The leader and two other birds dropped out of the flock. They skidded like ricocheting shot along the shore ice, all three dead.

"Can you get me some of that baking powder, Jimmy?" said Fred, slowly. "I, too, would like to make a bluebill kill in a 70-mile wind."

Roger Preus

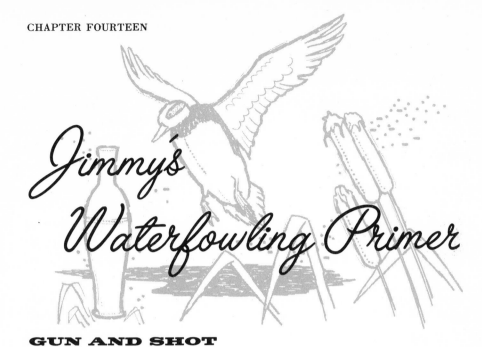

CHAPTER FOURTEEN

Jimmy's Waterfowling Primer

GUN AND SHOT

Every new convert to game bird shooting is faced with the problem of selecting the best gun for waterfowl and upland game birds. Too many make the mistake of acquiring a full-choke gun when they should use a modified or improved cylinder capable of throwing a wide, killing pattern at the ranges they can hit game. Most game birds are killed at ranges of twenty to thirty-five yards.

A full-choke shotgun is bored to deliver seventy to seventy-five per cent of the charge into a 30-inch circle at forty yards. When the range is less than forty yards the diameter of the pattern naturally becomes smaller and there is little margin for error by the untrained gunner.

Just under full choke is the improved modified choke. It is a compromise and is too close to the full choke to make any appreciable difference. The modified choke will put sixty per cent of the pellets into a 30-inch circle at forty yards—improved cylinder about fifty-five per cent and cylinder about fifty per cent. So there you have the pattern designations. Choose a shotgun capable of delivering a fairly open pattern and use the tight choke only when you become expert and have the need for it.

It is highly desirable to see for yourself just what your shotgun will do. The answer is always in the pattern board. Set up a paper target about four feet square. Fire a shot at the mark in the center of the paper from a distance of forty yards. Draw a 30-inch circle to encompass the greatest number of shot holes. The number of a certain size of shot in an ounce is readily available so that the number of shot holes within the circle can be counted and the percentage easily computed.

Guns vary in their ability to handle certain sizes of shot. One gun may pattern No. 6 shot perfectly and deliver a poor, spotty pattern when fed No. 4 shot. Even the same size shot in a different make of shell can produce a very different pattern. Your shotgun may have an affinity for a certain size of shot in a certain make and the pattern board will correctly prescribe the proper ammunition for your particular shotgun. Ammunition has gradually improved over the years and the modified choked gun made years ago is fully capable of delivering a better pattern than a full choke using ammunition made a decade ago.

If your gun will handle No. 6 shot well, you are fortunate, for this size is your best all-around load, but it will be far better to use No. 4s or 5s and enjoy a good pattern if your shotgun will not tolerate No. 6s. A fine, even pattern is a killing pattern and many misses and cripples can result when a gun throws a pattern with large holes in it. It takes about five pellets to kill a duck and a duck without feathers is a mighty small target. Pattern is of the greatest importance.

Will a 32-inch barrel shoot farther than a 30-inch barrel? For all practical purposes, there is very little difference in the ballistic results obtained from very short and very long barrels, with our modern powders. A 26-inch full-choke barrel may shoot just as hard and give as good a pattern as the 32-inch full-choke barrel, if the load used in both barrels is the same. Barrel lengths of thirty and thirty-two inches are usually used for trap and waterfowl gunning because of their longer sighting plane, making pointing more accurate.

Gail Evans, director of sales, Remington Arms, says, "Barrel lengths of twenty-six and twenty-eight inches are generally used for upland shooting and skeet, and these barrels usually are choked cylinder, modified or special skeet boring. They handle faster and the more

224

open pattern is desirable for short range shooting. They are also used effectively in decoy shooting."

I would suggest that a beginner start out with a 12-gauge. He won't have to worry about the recoil if he will use a pad and a light load. If you find that your gun is shooting over your birds, the gun stock is too straight. If you shoot under your target, the gun has too much drop.

Jack Mitchell, a fine duck shot who knows his shotgun, says, "I believe the novice hunter should use a 12-gauge with a modified choke. The average upland game bird is killed at twenty to twenty-five yards or less. The tighter the choke, the smaller the pattern. Consequently the full-choke shotgun is not advisable for the novice. If you use a full-choke on upland birds at short ranges, the game is ruined. With a modified choke, and the proper size of shot, any average game can be hit with sufficient pellets to bring it down up to forty yards. With a modified choke gun, the shooter has a larger killing pattern at this distance and will, therefore, get more game per shot."

During World War II I spent considerable time at army and air force camps. Captain Sam Nickerson of Boston, a skeet instructor at Harlington, Texas, Air Force base, put hundreds of recruits through the mill when I was there. Sam, one of the top ballistic men in my book, recommends a modified choke for the beginner, too.

"Many less experienced shooters are sold on a long barrel and full choke, but the shooter of long experience knows that the average man with this equipment is handicapped," he says. "For average shooting, the novice gunner should use a double gun with 28- or 30-inch barrels, bored improved cylinder or modified. If he shoots a repeater or automatic, it should have a 26- to 28-inch barrel bored modified."

I would suggest No. 6 shot for the average shooting on pheasants. When the shooting is at thirty yards or less, I would choose No. 7½ shot in a heavy load. Don't forget that, in shooting at a cross-flying pheasant, the last half of the total length of the bird is tail. The vital spots are in the head and the first one-quarter of the bird's length. The pheasant is a big bird and flies much faster than you think, so it is a good policy to figure out how much lead you should give him and then lead a little more. Late in the fall or winter, use a full choke and No. 4 shot, for the birds are wilder and ranges longer.

Pretty Loral I. Armstrong, duck hunting with her famous labrador Hi Hat Lady near her father's dog ranch, Anoka, Minnesota. Loral, a dog trainer for 14 years has a dog act in Nick Kahler's Sportsmen's show. An all-around sportswoman, she took a seven-point buck with a bow and arrow last fall and won the 1957 Minnesota state women's handicap trapshooting title.

Eddie Long likes a light Aluma Craft duck boat which he can drag into his blind with one hand.

Photo by Don Berg, Minneapolis

For the novice gunner, the same gun rules should apply to duck hunting. He should realize his shortcomings and lay off the long shot. If he shoots a gun with a single barrel, it should be bored modified. This would give a sixty per cent pattern in a 30-inch circle at forty yards, as I have stated. The novice has need of a large killing pattern when shooting over decoys. He will kill more birds with a modified than a full choke. If shooting a double gun over decoys at forty yards or less, one barrel should be modified and the other full choke. Be sure that you use the modified on the first shot.

For teal and decoy shooting I recommend No. 7½ shot. For all other ducks than teal, use No. 6 shot. The average hunter uses No. 6

shot for pass shooting and No. 4 shot is best for the large birds at long range. For goose shooting, use No. 4 shot.

Bill Weiss, New York, an internationally-known sportsman, has hunted everywhere. "I use No. 4 shot for geese, but carry along a few No. 2s for long shots," he said. "I shoot No. 2s only if I am in a position to retrieve crippled birds. Our goose shooting on the east coast is unlike your western field shooting where you wait until you see the white of their eyes," he added. "Most of our shots are long range and here is where the No. 2 plays a part, but you are more liable to wound your goose with the larger shot."

Magnum guns designated to handle the three-inch shells are not for the average duck hunter. Since the advent of the little magnum with its $1\frac{1}{2}$ oz. of shot in the $2\frac{3}{4}$ case, the hunters who felt that they needed fire power have switched over to the more comfortable shell and seem more willing to allow the few who can handle the long Roman Candles for pass and goose shooting to take the punishment.

Actually, the regular heavy duck load will work wonders if the gun is pointed properly. Even the three-inch shell will only kill about five yards farther. No. 6 shot has the happy faculty of losing its killing pattern and its penetrating ability at about the same range. No. 4 shot will get out a longer distance but the five pellets necessary to bring a duck down dead may not be a part of the killing pattern and a cripple results. I think that the greatest advantage in the use of the magnum is the increased number of shot that can be had in a larger pattern at a given range. In other words, a modified barrel will do a mighty good job at full-choke range if the shell is loaded with an extra one-fourth or more ounces of a certain size of shot.

Duck hunters with but one gun would do well to consider a variable choke device on their pumps and auto loaders. These gadgets are becoming increasingly popular. Like Ernie Simmons of Kansas City, the famous gun expert, says, "With a simple twist or a change of tubes my skeet gun can become my duck gun." The compensator type will reduce recoil but there is a blasting effect that is not too easy on the ears of a companion in a duck blind or shooting at the trap, but thousands of the top gun handlers in skeet will testify to the efficiency of the variable chokes.

228

DUCK BOATS AND EQUIPMENT

No man on water is safer than the boat that floats him. Yet I have seen duck hunters venture forth in contraptions held together by bailing wire and adhesive tape. Every fall scores of waterfowlers lose their lives in hunting accidents on water, and a major cause is a faulty boat. Most of the victims were guilty of criminal negligence for taking such craft out in the first place.

And the loss of life is so needless, for the sporting goods stores of the nation are crammed with good, safe duck boats in aluminum, wood, canvas, and even steel. They are designed and built with safety as a prime requisite.

Most duck hunting accidents on water begin with a nimrod's desire to economize by building his own duck boat or buying a homemade affair that will at least make shift for him. But it's poor economy. Most of these "built it myself" marvels have a way of working apart at the seams; they can't take the pounding of waves and ice, and they require a major overhaul every season.

Several years ago Charlie Johnson, Minneapolis sports editor, Marc Wenner, noted sportsman, and I were hunting ducks at Clayt Peterson's camp on Dead Lake in northern Minnesota. We watched two eager hunters pull out from the dock about two hours before the noon opening.

Suddenly we heard one of them hollering for help and we could see that their boat was sinking. Luckily they had life preservers and were able to make it back to the shore. But they lost their guns, shells and the boat. They hadn't even thought to test their boat in water before hauling it two hundred miles to their hunting site.

If your boat is a wooden one, be sure to caulk it and paint it in mid-summer when it has thoroughly dried out. Then, before the season opening, soak it a few days under water. This will swell the joints and make it watertight. If you do any hunting after the freeze-up, be sure to cover the bow and bottom of the boat with tin so the sharp edges of ice can't chew into the wood.

During and since World War II, rapid strides were made in developing caulking compounds. A concentrated marine boat cement and crack repairer, now on the market, was used on such crafts as the famous

PT boats. This compound will caulk seams as wide as half an inch. This filler is absolutely waterproof and much better than the old method of rags (or cotton twist) and tar, which I used for many years.

Fiber-glass cloth, a new development, is also good. Cover your boat with fiber glass and you'll be sure of a lifetime job. It won't rot, can't leak and you don't have to worry about painting your boat year after year.

Your oars should be in good condition, and it is wise to take a push-paddle along. I always carry an extra paddle in my duckboat. Take along some clothesline and string—you'll find it will come in handy when you're tying your boat to the rushes. The man who hunts much should own his boat and trailer. Very few duck camps have reliable boats and often your duck shoot is ruined by a leaky boat or a gaudily painted fishing boat. A duckboat takes more rough abuse during the duck season than a fishing boat does all summer so don't expect the duck club owner to have a new boat for hire. Light boats are fine, but don't overload them or go out in a heavy sea. Light duckboats are desirable for marsh shooting but very dangerous for lake shooting.

Be sure your shell box is waterproof and that you have plenty of dry matches and a screwdriver in case your gun breaks down. I always make it a point to have a couple of sacks of dry hay in my boat.

Dress well and be prepared for any kind of weather—severe cold, wet or warm. Often it may be warm in the morning and turn severely cold with rain (or snow) in the afternoon. You should always wear woolen underwear, regardless of how warm it may be when you start out. Several years ago a number of hunters were trapped in the terrific Armistice Day storm which swept over Minnesota and neighboring states. Many lives were lost when the summer-like weather suddenly turned into a raging blizzard and caught hunters in light underwear and shirt sleeves. An extra pair of socks, two pair of warm gloves or mittens, a rainproof jacket, two suits of underwear, hunting coat, rubber boots, two wool shirts and miscellaneous other warm and waterproof clothing will go easily into your duffel bag. If you use rubber hip boots, get yourself a pair of leather or web boot suspenders. Boot straps fastened to your pants belt constantly pull your pants downward, making you uncomfortable.

Take along an extra shotgun of the same gauge, if you possibly can; for one may break and spoil your hunting trip. Be sure you do

Guides Speed Lavalle and Rod Ducharme, with Joe Brush, Ted Culbertson and Chuck Murphy, and the author sitting with Walt Taylor. Our old duck club on Lake Manitoba in 1936.

not have any 20-gauge shells in your pockets if you are hunting with a 12-gauge. They may get mixed up and cause you serious trouble. Don't get any three-inch shells mixed up with your regular loads. You will have trouble if, by mistake, you place one of them in the magazine of your pump or automatic. Don't have your gun loaded when setting out your decoys or when moving from one spot to another.

Wipe off your gun each night with an oily rag when you come in from the duck marsh; otherwise it may rust. Take along a thermos jug with hot coffee, soup or tea. Be sure you have a roll of tape in your kit. You can use it to tape up a sore finger or to fasten the recoil pad to your gun if it gets loose.

Use heavy, dark-colored cord for your decoys. Fishlines, often used by hunters, or light string will tangle and cause you plenty of trouble.

No hunter should be without a good knife. It is one of the most useful tools in your equipment bag. I am never without my sleeping bag on any kind of hunt. You are always sure of having a good rest if you have your sleeping bag in your car. Be sure your clothing, especially the hunting cap and coat, blends with the cover in which you shoot. Wear a woolen muffler. It is a warm addition to the hunter's wardrobe; if the weather is mild, a silk scarf will save a lot of neck chafing.

*   *   *   *

DUCK BLINDS

Ducks, and all other waterfowl, have far better eyesight than man when it comes to detecting movements or unfamiliar objects. So it's absolutely necessary for the hunter to camouflage himself with some material that will break up his outline and conceal him if his decoys are to do their most effective job of attracting birds into gun range.

Hence a duck blind to hide the hunter is one of the most essential parts of the duck hunter's equipment. And the best duck blind of all is the one made from the natural vegetation or other materials at hand where the decoy spread is set.

Jules Greiner, one of the best duck blind builders I know in the northwest, has often said, "A flock of fifty ducks has a hundred eyes and they are constantly on the lookout for danger. From their vantage point in the sky they can detect any slight unnatural movement on the ground. Just move a hair and the old greenhead mallard will flare and keep out of gun range." The redhead duck is about the only duck I know that is careless. I have seen bluebills and canvasbacks decoy easily on a dull stormy day, but usually ducks of any kind are wary. A good hide is essential.

Build your blind so it will blend with the surroundings. It should resemble natural cover and be constructed of materials native to the spot. If you are going to shoot in rushes, select the thickest clump in the line of flight and push your boat in at right angles to the flyway. Be sure to hide the end of your boat that is closest to the open water. Often, the hunter shoves in his boat but leaves the space behind him uncovered. You can close up the opening by cutting a few rushes and use them to conceal the other end of your boat.

Be careful that you don't build your blind so high it will hinder your shooting. When in rushes break off the tops of the stems so you can swing your gun freely. After you have built your blind sit down and wait for the ducks. Don't keep popping your head up when you sight a flock. If you happen to be standing when ducks come in, keep perfectly still. Don't move a muscle or the flock will flare out of range.

When shooting in fields remember that mallards feed mostly by day, arriving usually in the early morning or at dawn. They are very wary, and will circle several times before they light. Build yourself a hide from grain or corn shocks in a field where they have been feeding. Be sure you don't disturb the surroundings. Some hunters dig pits in the fields and place out decoys. I have found this the most effective way to hunt those curly-tailed mallards.

Mallards will work all day if the weather is rough and stormy, but they are hard to bring within gunshot on a warm, clear day.

Remember that ducks above you can see down into your blind. Stay in the shadow as your upturned white face will give you away in spite of the best blind you can construct.

I have shot ducks from blinds made of rushes in western Canada, from platforms in trees in Arkansas, from pits in the Dakotas and Minnesota, from blinds made of logs on the Illinois River, from drift-wood hides in Louisiana, and from tule blinds in California, and I

Trees served as blinds in Arkansas when I hunted with Ted Williams, Boston Red Sox slugger and Eddie Lopat of the New York Yankees.

Photo by Dr. Drennen, Stuttgart

A black duck blind on one of the many duck ponds on Maryland's Eastern shore.

Photo by John Scott

A dry comfortable blind on a Minnesota lake.

Photo by Don Berg, Minneapolis

have come to the conclusion that all blinds must carefully fit the natural surroundings.

I have had some great shoots on Chesapeake Bay in Maryland, out in open water miles from shore. Typical offshore blind is a wooden box erected on stilts and covered with pine bows. A slip in the rear hides the duck boat. Inside, a bench and racks for guns and shells allows the gunners to relax when the birds are not flying. Several dozen decoys, yes, even up to two or three hundred, are spread out in front,

A Porto-Blind is wind proof and waterproof and weighs just eighteen pounds. It holds two hunters and can be used for ducks or deer hunting.

mostly cans and some bluebills. These blinds would not work in other localities. They are permanent and the ducks have become used to them.

Back in the marsh, two-man blinds of woven marsh grass are placed near a pond for black duck. Take a dozen decoys, a good caller, a good retriever, and you're in business. Empty shells, brightly colored shell boxes, any object which shines, or doesn't fit naturally around your hide, should be removed.

Jack Seville and the author watching a flock of cans.

Photo by John Scott

DUCK DECOYS

Decoys are an important part of your duck-hunting equipment. The more good decoys you have in front of your blind, properly placed, the better chance there will be of bringing ducks within range. There is one exception, however—it is when you are shooting over a small pothole. Five or ten decoys in this case are sufficient.

Ducks do not like wind or stormy weather. They prefer lee shores. However, I have shot ducks on the windy side of a lake when they were after a certain kind of feed. The first thing you should do in the morning is to find out which way the wind is blowing. If it is blowing from the south, hunt on the south side of the lake or marsh. If it is blowing from the north, chances are the ducks will work on that side of the water, out of the wind. This is the place to set out your blocks. If the wind changes, change your location as well.

Poor decoys are a handicap in themselves. When they are not smartly placed the chance of a successful hunt is much reduced. If a hunter knows the most effective arrangement of decoys, he can insist upon his guide placing them that way.

It is cold out there in the morning and the easy thing is to heave just a few blocks in the water near the blind. The more decoys you throw out, the more you will have to pick up when your shoot has ended—but that's the way it must be done. The good hunter will take time to place enough decoys in the right way, and he will enjoy better hunting.

Your duck decoys should look natural. You can't expect to decoy mallards with canvasback decoys, or bluebills with pintail decoys. Naturally, diver ducks, such as bluebills (scaup), canvasbacks and redheads, will decoy to their kind. You'll find puddle ducks, such as spoonbills, mallards, pintails, etc., decoying more readily to their own kind, too.

Locate the feeding grounds of the ducks. You'll find that the deep-diving ducks feed in deeper water than the puddlers. Don't place your canvasback or redhead decoys in shallow water. Ducks can see the bottom from the air—and the divers aren't interested in shallow feeding.

The reverse applies to puddle ducks, such as mallards and pintails. It would be folly to set out dipper decoys in deep water. These ducks feed only in shallow water.

Only a few decoys are needed for local ducks early in the season, but your stool should be increased as the season advances. Early in the season, leave your brightly painted decoys at home, and put your faith in dull-painted hens. Use your bright decoys when the northern birds come down. They have much more color.

All ducks, as a rule, light and take off against the wind—like a plane. This is true of the deep-water divers as well as the mallards, but some of the other dippers do, on occasion, make a cross-wind landing. A wind at right angles to the blind is the ideal wind, and what a help that can be if it blows your dead ducks against a shore not too far away. Second choice is the wind that comes from your back or over your shoulder. Beware of the wind that blows in your face, as the ducks will not swing over your blind to come in to your decoys.

Bluebills, canvasbacks and redheads, all divers, will cross over your decoys and light inside. So it is well to place your diver decoys about thirty-five yards out from your blind. The dipper ducks will be inclined to keep to the outside of your stool, so bring your mallard decoys in a lot closer. String out the diver decoys so they are not too close to each other, but the mallards can be bunched.

There are times when ducks do not decoy, regardless of how many decoys you have or how good they are. This happened to me last fall when I was hunting canvasbacks up on the famous Delta Marshes with Grady Clark and Bill Figge, two top duck hunters. On that day the cans were paying no attention to our twenty decoys which we had scattered in front of our blind. I determined to find the reason. I picked up a dozen of the decoys and strung them out in a straight line onto the marsh beyond the stool. The last decoy was about a hundred yards from our blind. At first a few, then more canvasbacks, started to work into our decoys. Apparently they had not seen the blocks before.

Ducks always spread out when they feed. They don't assume a military formation. Keep this in mind and have your decoys look as natural as possible.

Dave Ramsey, one of my favorite hunting companions, who would rather hunt ducks than eat, prefers the triangle system of placing decoys, and it has worked successfully for him. Placing the triangle for-

Decoy making, an art that once flourished in the Chesapeake Bay area in Maryland. With a block of wood, a hatchet and a sharp knife, Clayton Creighton of Hopper's Island, Maryland, can produce a decoy in a few minutes.

Bill Rivere, Herters' Research expert, skins a mallard to make a feathered decoy.

mation differs for dippers and divers. For dippers with a wind blowing at right angle to the blind, two triangular bunches of mallard decoys are placed about twenty-five yards upwind from the blind and not too far out, with the bases of the triangles parallel to the shore. The points of the triangles are thus quite a way out but this distance is dependent upon the number of blocks used. A nice wide lane is left between the two triangular groups and two attractive mallard hen blocks and a feeder block are spotted all by themselves opposite the lane between the two groups—and not more than about fifteen yards from the blind. In others words the latter group is midway between the bases of the triangles and between them and the shore. This is a beautiful setup for dipper ducks—the dippers will tend to light in front of the blind.

If it's divers some radical changes must be made in the triangle formation. The two triangular bunches are set out downwind, and the points of the triangles are reversed, now pointing toward the blind, with the bases on the far side. A lane through the two groups is left as before, and two canvasback or bluebill decoys are spotted in front of the blind in line with the middle of the land. The points of the triangles are about fifteen yards from the blind. The divers will come smack down the lane to the opening in front of the blind.

A few coot decoys (black blocks) and a couple of goose decoys are great pullers. You can't put out too many decoys (except when shooting in a pothole). If the water is calm, tie a string around one of your decoys and jerk it to cause the water to ripple. On still days, the ducks look for ripples on water caused by feeding ducks. If you are shooting in the timber, climb down from your blind and make a "splash" in the water. I first learned this little quirk in Arkansas. I was hunting with Win Stephens, Jr., and Floyd Whitaker near Stuttgart. The mallards were driving into the pin oaks like mad, but evading our decoys. But when more incoming flocks heard the splash they swung within gun range of our blind.

There are many ways of placing out decoys. If you are wrong, it won't take you long to correct your stool. But always bear in mind—watch where the ducks are working and you will find this the best place to set out your blocks.

DUCK CALLING

The duck hunter who has never learned to use a call is missing one of the real thrills of the sport and is handicapping himself unnessarily. It is true that ducks often will come into a stool of decoys without any calling whatsoever. But sometime during every season there comes a day when ducks respond poorly or not at all to decoys. On such days a call, judiciously used, will bring ducks in when nothing else can.

Some years ago live decoys were permissible, but their devastating effectiveness necessitated their eventual banning by law. What made them so much more effective than inanimate decoys was the babbling of hen mallards in front of a blind. They had a way of coaxing every passing flock into the range of the gunner.

Now that live decoys have been banned, the hunter still can have a lot of fun fooling a flock of ducks with a duck call. There is a lot of satisfaction in being able to swing a flock headed in another direction into your stool of decoys. But to do these things, both the caller and the duck call must be good.

Years ago I developed more than one headache carting around a bunch of live decoys. I had to feed and take care of them as I would my hunting dog, and about all they did during the non-hunting months was eat. A good duck call costing a few dollars is far better. Duck calling has become a part of the hunt. I own several duck calls, but am still not an expert caller although I have a pretty good idea of what good calling is when I hear it. I have been a judge at the national duck calling contest at Stuttgart, Arkansas, on several different occasions.

Although duck calls have found a ready sale among hunters, they have, in most cases, been of more help to the ducks than to the hunter. You must have a duck call that sounds "ducky" and be able to use it well. Otherwise, don't use it at all.

It takes hours of practice to become a good duck caller. I know hunters who carry a duck call wherever they go throughout the year. Lyle Wright, one of my hunting buddies, who has developed into a good caller, carries his call in his car and practices daily when driving around the country. Said Lyle, "Get in as much practice as you can

Stuttgart, Arkansas, features the annual national duck-calling championships. Judges (left to right) Bill Tanner; Nash Buckingham, author; Bob Becker, out door editor of the Chicago Tribune; the late Wallace Berry, movie actor; Jimmy Robinson; and Lynn Bogue Hunt, famed waterfowl artist.

when driving. You won't bother anybody and the practice will pay off handsomely in the duck season. Even the best call is worthless if you don't know how to blow it well."

I contend you can do a bang-up job of duck calling if you master only four calls. These are mallard calls which will attract all the dipper ducks, such as pintails, teal, and widgeons. The divers, such as bluebills, canvasbacks and redheads, won't answer to these calls.

The "hi-bawl" is a loud, long call used to attract high-flying flocks and call their attention to your decoys. This call is unusual because it is never made by a duck. It sounds probably like a big gab-

Ralph True, professional duck caller, demonstrates the comeback call.

bling flock of birds far off. At any rate, it is effective in accomplishing its purpose. After the attention of the flock is secured, and they break and start for your stool, use the "greeting" or "feed" call. When ducks are close in, start to "chuckle." Keep up this fast, soft call until you are ready to shoot. If the flock starts away, use the "come-back" call and as soon as they turn toward you switch back to the "chuckle."

Calling conditions vary in different localities. Use the calls that the native residents have found effective, because these have been learned by hard experience. The lay of the land around a hunting spot can cause echoes which will scare ducks—if certain calls are used.

I can't tell you, in print, how to make these calls. You will have to learn from a good caller or phonograph record. Learn to make a long *quack;* if you practice this until it sounds like an old mallard hen the other calls will come easily—after you have heard them.

Most men attempt to blow into a duck call. It isn't done that way. The effort must come from the muscles of the diaphragm. Divide the sound *quack* into two syllables like this, *qu-ack*. Now say it and then try it again without moving the lips. That's the way a duck call is "blown."

Anyone can learn to call divers. Some days they will decoy into anything. The bluebills, cans and redheads don't call. They make a purring sound. You can imitate this with a duck call by recalling a trill you probably made as a kid. This trill is made by fluttering the tip of the tongue as the breath is expelled. Now put the call to your lips and do it. *Brrrrrr, brrrrrr, brrrrrrr.* Learn to do this and you will do well with the divers. It isn't hard to do, but few know the stunt.

Goose calling requires a special goose call, although some call the Canada and blue goose by mouth. Goose calls are much easier to learn than duck calls, since the call has two tones and does not require long practice to attain reasonable proficiency.

* * * *

HUNTING DOGS

A dog, man's best friend, is also his best ally in his conservation efforts. It would be hard to estimate the value of a good hunting dog in dollars and cents. Dogs recover hundreds of thousands of game birds each year which otherwise would be lost. Take ducks, for example. It is estimated that hunters cripple and lose twenty-five per cent of their ducks and I think this estimate is low. This means that approximately five million downed ducks are lost each year, and a big percentage of them could have been recovered by good dogs. I hate to think of how many pheasants are crippled and lost each year. They, too, could have been recovered by a good retriever.

In every section of the country you'll find the guy who lays claim to having the best hunting dog in the world. I like this kind of a fellow. I know that when he says this he loves that dog and has spent many long hours training him.

My friend, Henry P. Davis, world's greatest dog authority, field trial judge and writer, says, "There are three kinds of hunters; one, the fellow who hunts without a dog; two, one who hunts with a dog he owns himself or with a companion who owns a dog; and three, the chap who hunts with a dog he raised and trained himself.

"The hunter who goes afield without a dog can have a lot of fun . . . but he misses a lot, too. The fellow who hunts with a trained dog he has purchased or with a friend's good hunting dog will get far more pleasure out of his trips afield and bag a greater share of game. But the sportsman who hunts with the dog he has developed himself is the one who is reaping the full measure of thrills from his day's jaunt in the open."

Given the right material and using a fair amount of judgment, the task of training a hunting dog is not really a hard one. On the other hand it can, and should be, a lot of fun. There are a number of good books on dog training, any one of which can direct the sportsman on the right path to teaching the fundamentals. By following these instructions the dog owner can develop almost any well-bred young hunting dog that shows promise into an obedient and effective gunning asset that can give him thrills and pleasure he can derive from no other source.

In choosing a hunting dog prospect, regardless of breed or type, pointing dog, retriever or hound, it is best to look into its ancestry. This does not mean that a full line of champions is necessary to a good pedigree. But the young dog that comes from stock that is well known for its hunting ability is much more apt to inherit a keen desire to hunt than one which stems from a line that has not been used for hunting purposes for generations. Be sure that the mother and father of your prospect are good hunters themselves. If possible, see them work in the field. This is important, although it is no sure guarantee that your young dog will turn out as well. It is too much to expect that *all* well-bred young hunting dogs will develop into top performers in the field, but good breeding is a mighty fine background. As H. P. "Skog" Skoglund, well-known insurance executive who has hunted ducks in Minnesota for forty years, says, "Blood will tell." This rule is not infallible, but it is a pretty safe rule to hang your hat on when it comes to hunting dogs.

Woodcock shooting in Maine with Jack Boone and Harry Nelson.

Don't try to make a jack-of-all-trades out of your hunting dog. All sporting dogs are specialists on one or more types of game, and while all are versatile in a high degree, none can turn in a top-notch job on all types of upland game and waterfowl. Sure, all of us have seen remarkable examples of gun dog versatility. For instance, I have seen hounds retrieve upland game birds and waterfowl. Bassets and beagles often are good retrievers of game birds. "I've seen a springer spaniel tree coons, not once but regularly," said Henry Davis.

So decide what type of hunting you most prefer and get a dog from a breed that was specially developed to work on the kind of game you hunt most. Then point your training program toward developing him into the finest sort of gun aid in that particular type of hunting and let the extra curricular activities take care of themselves.

Don't expect to develop a young dog into a finished performer overnight. It takes real field experience, and a lot of it, to make a top gun dog, but you can give him a mighty good start by teaching him the proper manners and the necessary degree of obedience. Don't try to push him along too fast, even though he might show unusual promise and seems to learn readily. Take it easy with him, in short lessons, and you'll find they'll stay with him longer and, instead of becoming a matter of drudgery, his training sessions will be sort of an enjoyable game to him.

There are many good books on dog training. Get the book to fit the type of dog you wish to train. Read it thoroughly and pay attention to what you read. Then study the characteristics of your pupil. Some dogs take correction cheerfully, others that are more timid must be handled with care. The latter type must be taken along slowly, without any attempt to force them. If too much force is applied or stern methods of correction are used, the trainer runs the risk of breaking the dog's spirit and creating a situation that may be impossible to clear up.

What is the right age to start training a dog? Many trainers disagree. Some favor starting with the bare fundamentals at a very early age, others prefer to wait until the dog has reached a more mature age when he can better absorb what the trainer is trying to teach. Nine or ten months might be closest to the right answer. At that time you can get an idea concerning his hunting desire which is the most important factor in the make-up of a gun dog. Expose the youngster to the open fields for a number of times, letting him accompany an older dog at first. Don't expect him to break out and range all over the countryside searching game the first few times out, for all this will be new to him. If he shows some signs of an inquisitive nature, this is all to the good. And so much the better if he evidences a bold nature. After a few trips, should he show a keen desire to get out and search the cover, even though he does not know what he's searching for, he is showing promise, for unless he possesses a keen hunting desire, all your training efforts will be wasted. The one thing a trainer cannot make a dog do is hunt. Certainly he can be forced to range out and make impressive casts, but if he isn't possessed of a great desire to actually hunt for game, he is practically worthless. He may be quite headstrong in his desire to cover the country, but this can be controlled in time. If, however, he shows no desire to get out from under your feet after you have taken him afield a few times and he has seen other dogs enjoying themselves in the activity for which they were bred, it will be best to discard him and start afresh with a better prospect.

Control, in varying degrees, is essential in the training of every type of hunting dog, including fox and coon hounds. The unruly dog can ruin many a hunt, while the dog that is under his master's control is indeed a joy to hunt with.

It is not too difficult to effect control. And it is not necessary to exercise force to bring the dog under complete command. But it does often require a considerable amount of patience and this is one quality which every man who trains a dog must continually exercise. Control through kindness is much more effective and lasting than control through fear, and it can be brought about without causing the dog to lose any of his independence on his hunting desire. Correction, at times, is, of course, necessary but firmness can be administered without brutality and both man and dog will feel better for it. Teach the young dog the meaning of the word "Whoa," and have him obey it instantly. This is the most important word in the dog trainer's vocabulary. Use it sparingly but enforce it when you use it. This brings the dog to a quick stop regardless of what he is doing. If you can create a willingness on his part to obey this command promptly every time it is given, you will have gone a long way toward directing his energies in the right channel and you'll always have him under control.

Watch out for gun shyness. This is a preventable fault that, once acquired, is often hard to cure. Acquaint the dog with gunfire at an early age. If you start with a puppy, pop a cap pistol around him at meal time. Do this only at meal time so he will associate the noise with his regular feeding period. Then as he becomes completely inured to the noise or looks forward to it with eagerness, gradually increase it with a .22 cartridge, a .410 shotgun, then a 20-gauge and finally a twelve. Do not shoot directly over the puppy's head.

If you are choosing a young dog, make sure he is not gun shy before you buy him. If he has never heard firearms, start him out as you did the puppy. If he is timid, don't buy him. Pick your prospect carefully. See that he comes from a good stock, has a bold disposition, shows a keen interest in hunting and is normally healthy. Then you have something to work on. Then follow your book. Then you'll have the time of your life in training your own hunting dog.

Great attention should be given the dog's food. Changes in food affect him in the same way they do his master. Poor food and bad quarters are the chief causes of dogs losing flesh so rapidly when they are on a hunt in strange country. Proper food should be shipped with the dog. Feed two hours before the hunt; dry food is best. It won't hurt to give the dog a warm meal in the evening and a good rubdown. If his feet are sore, bathe them with hot water and witch hazel. My good friend, Wally Walters, a real friend of hunting dogs, claims that most puppies have worms. "But," said Wally, "that doesn't mean that every owner of a new puppy should buy worm medicince. It is best to consult a veterinarian." Among the most common symptoms of worms in puppies are: enormous or finicky appetites; a harsh unthrifty coat that lacks sheen; loss of weight; a soft hacking cough and watery eyes.

Although distemper occurs most frequently in young dogs, all dogs are susceptible, especially those under a year old. Keep your dog in good physical condition, then if distemper strikes he may be able to defeat the disease with the help of a vet. If your dog loses pep, doesn't want to play, becomes very sluggish, won't eat, and generally doesn't look or act right, better take him to the doctor because distemper often starts with these symptoms. The easiest way to prevent distemper is to have a vet inoculate your puppy.

HOW TO BAG DUCKS

Ducks have never been trained so they will follow a fixed program when they are coming in on the hunter. They may come in high, and drop down rapidly, or they may come in low, from behind, from in front, from the side; or they may circle and look the situation over carefully. It all depends.

Duck shooting over a pass is the most difficult form of shooting. If you are missing your ducks here, the chances are you are shooting behind them. Last fall I was shooting with Elton Hess and Bernie Hanson on a pass with the wind blowing up to forty miles an hour. The boys were having trouble and Elton asked, "Jimmy, how much should I lead these bloody ducks?" "Shove your gun farther ahead of them," I said. "Keep moving with the bird, don't stop your gun." I have taught hundreds of hunters how to lead ducks over a pass and I doubt if any one of them had been leading his ducks too far. Ninety-nine times out of a hundred the hunter is shooting directly at the ducks or leading them only a few feet. As a result, his shot string is actually several feet behind the fast-flying bird he pointed at.

Always remember that ducks can fly about eighty feet in a second. This means they can fly twenty or more feet in the fraction of a second it takes to press the trigger of your shotgun. Therefore, take a big lead on your ducks and the chances are you will have better results when shooting on a pass.

Fred Etchen, all-American trapshooter, famous field shot and shotgun instructor, has taught more people how to shoot than any other man. My old duck camp on Lake Manitoba was one of Fred's and his son Rudy's favorite shooting spots. One day when Fred and I were shooting canvasbacks on our duck pass, I asked, "What is the first thing you teach a new shooter, Fred?"

"Follow through," he said. "Follow through."

Take a good lead—that's the secret of hitting ducks. Jim Otis, an expert duck shot, says, "Lead the average duck by four feet at forty yards and you won't be far off."

There are times when I am off form and I start to check my gun and ammunition for an alibi. Then I start shoving my gun out in front of those ducks and immediately I get better results.

Decoy shooting is an altogether different story. I always remember what Bard Higgins, old time trapshot and duck student, used to say, "Speed is essential in decoy shooting. You don't have as much time to point your ducks as you do on a pass." This has been my experience. Not that it takes an expert shot to kill a duck that has settled his wings over the decoys. It does take a good shot to knock down a duck that is circling the decoys. On the latter, you get in front of your duck as you would in pass shooting. You must learn to lead the duck quickly to left or right if it swings. You must be alert in your duck blind and try to keep watch both in front and behind. How many times have you had a duck, or several of them, slip up behind you when you were gazing straight in front of your blind? I still have this happen to me.

The duck that bores down, or is flying toward you, is a different shot. He will be hard to hit if you shoot directly over your head at fifteen or twenty yards. Generally I jump up when an oncoming flock of low-flying ducks is fifty to sixty yards in front of me. Then they will put on the brakes, start climbing and I can get in my shots. Don't get excited and shoot at your duck if he is too close. Your pattern is very small at short range and if you hit him you'll blow him to bits.

Every duck hunter with any experience in the game likes to bag big ducks—canvasbacks, those big northern bluebills and fat prairie mallards. But what a surprise the big duck addict would get if he ever shot teal in Cuba or pen-raised mallards on Richard Mellon's fabulous Rolling Rock hunting club in Pennsylvania, near Pittsburgh. He would find sport equal to the best he had ever known on the prairies of Manitoba, Saskatchewan or Alberta.

Mallard shooting at the Mellon club, for instance, is a much sportier proposition than among the flooded oaks of Arkansas or on the stubble fields of North Dakota. The place is a 36,000-acre game paradise boasting deer, pheasants, wild turkeys, quail and even brook trout, in addition to the mallard setup.

It was built by Dick Mellon's father, Andrew Mellon, many years ago. He wanted a place for his friends to hunt. But they, hesitating about the annual infringement upon the elder Mellon's hospitality, virtually forced him to turn the property into a hunting club in which they could share the expenses.

A group of us having dinner in Richard Mellon's trophy room at his famous Rolling Rock Hunting club, near Pittsburgh. Rolling Rock is the most fabulous shooting club in the world.

I hunted there a couple of times, once with Don Knutson and Rog Kenna of New York, and was amazed at what the place had to offer. Its pheasant shooting over dogs was very similar to what you would find in South Dakota, but the mallard shooting was something I had never experienced before.

Don Knutson put it appropriately when he remarked, "I just couldn't believe that released mallards could give a man so much trouble."

254

On the property, at the foot of a big hill, was a lake on which the birds rested and fed. Each evening before a shoot game keepers would climb the hill with pens of mallards to be held all night so they would be hungry and eager to return to the lake. They were released at dawn and the hunters would be waiting in luxurious blinds half way to the lake.

Those mallards came down the hill at tree-top level like jet-propelled rockets. And I don't think I have ever had sportier shooting than we got there on Dick Mellon's Rolling Rock hunting acres.

Spencer Olin uses a straight stock when shooting mallards in the trees at his duck club near Stuttgart, Arkansas.

As for teal, I was like so many other duck hunters who pass them up for bigger ducks until I hunted in Cuba. I always argued, "Why waste a shell on anything smaller than a widgeon or a mallard?" Then one year I visited my friends Frankie and Olga Steinhart on their estate outside of Havana, Cuba. They are among the top live pigeon shots on the island, and in Europe.

Bob Naegele and I had been the Steinharts' guests for a live pigeon shoot at the Havana Gun Club and Frankie had lined up several of his friends for the shoot. Among them were Mungo Perez, who was widely known at Grand American trapshoots; the Villaba brothers and Armando Pessino of the Baccardi rum family, a famous hunter.

"Jimmy, why don't you and your friends take a day off and hunt teal with us?" Pessino said. "I know you've hunted ducks in Cuba before, but why not let your friends in for a good teal shoot?"

Naegele merely shook his head at the mention of teal. But I had known from a previous hunting experience with Homer Clark, the world's live pigeon champ, and Bill Isetts, that Cuban teal can be plenty tough. So I persuaded Naegele to try it with me the next day.

The hunters are set up in blinds built in trees about thirty feet off the ground. You have to crawl up a ladder to get in your blind. When everything is set, beaters stir up the teal on the adjoining sloughs and they come buzzing past your ears like arrows from a blowgun. Believe me, a 40-yard shot at a tiny teal zooming past your blind is a rough shot, as Naegele soon learned.

I don't think I've ever had tougher shots. You have to get out so far in front of your target that the lead is almost unbelievable.

For timber shooting, where the ducks are above the treetops, use a straight stock, if possible. Spencer Olin, Alton, Illinois, an ace duck shooter who shoots most of his ducks at wooded Stuttgart, Ark., has a stock as straight as a broom. The chances are that you will shoot under the ducks when you use a stock with too much drop in it.

Jump shooting is another favorite pastime of the duck hunter. It is best on calm days when the ducks are lying close in the marshes. Paddle your canoe quietly along the rushes and be ready for the big mallard when he swings into the air. Yes, you can miss this big duck very easily, and the chances are you have shot under him. He climbs at great speed, much faster than you think. Swing your gun high over him, and you will have more chance of hitting him. This is where that straight stock pays off.

Don't wait for your ducks to decoy unless you are a meat hunter. Give them a sporting chance. You will get more kick out of knocking down a double when ducks are passing over your head or outside your decoys.

Practice makes perfect. To be a good billiard, golf or baseball player requires hours of practice, as well as some natural ability. Some learn much faster than others. One man's reaction time is quick, another man's is slow. One hunter swings rapidly with his gun, another slowly. You must work these things out for yourself.

The trouble is that the average hunter shoots only about fifty shells a year, uses his gun only during the hunting season. Baseball, hockey, football and other sports have training periods. The hunter should train likewise at the trap and skeet field. Even the best trap and skeet shots spend hours of practice on the firing range. Bob Allen, world's doubles champ, Maynard Henry, a California duck hunter of note who holds the highest average ever attained on doubles targets, Fred Alford, Slim Oliver, Woody Woodcock, Roger Fawcett, Johnny Sternberger, Geo. Berkner, and a thousand other famous clay target shots, shoot up thousands of rounds of ammunition each year. They are all excellent field shots.

Timing and co-ordination are important, and you must be able to judge distance, if you expect to be a good shot, either at game or at clay targets. I often measure the distance from my blind to the farthest decoy. Thus I automatically have a good idea of the range when ducks come in.

How far do I lead a duck? Frankly, I don't know how much I lead a bird, so how can I tell you? That is something each shooter must learn to judge for himself. How can I tell you to lead a duck when I don't know how fast that duck is flying or at what angle? Some ducks loaf along the slough, maybe looking for feed, at thirty miles an hour. Others sweep down the lake at sixty miles an hour, maybe ninety with a stiff breeze behind. If this is the case, how can anybody tell you how far to lead a duck? You must figure out the lead yourself. If you are missing, just increase your lead.

I do believe in shotgun instructors. They can tell you if your gun fits you after you have shot a few rounds, and if it doesn't how to

257

correct it. They can correct your stance and give you other valuable tips that will help you in the field. After you have had this instruction, the rest is up to you. I advise all young shooters to try a few rounds at skeet or traps. Harold Russell, Minneapolis All-American skeet gunner and instructor, will say, "I will guarantee a novice hunter will kill twice as many ducks this fall if he shoots just a case of shells (500) at traps or skeet before the hunting season opens."

A common fault with many hunters is that they pull up and "bang" when a pheasant or duck flushes. They don't take time out to point their bird. This generally results in a miss or a crippled bird. You should be calm at all times and point out your bird before pressing the trigger. Don't let the bird bluff you into shooting too fast.

The fit of a shotgun is as important as the fit of your hat. You may be using a shotgun with too much drop in the stock. The mediocre shot should use a modified or improved-cylinder choke instead of a full choke. On chokes, Dave Yaeger, ballistics expert of the Federal Cartridge company at Anoka, gave us these figures. Said Dave, "A full choke gun will put between seventy and seventy-five per cent of its shot charge in a 30-inch circle at forty yards while a modified is sixty to sixty-five per cent and the improved cylinder fifty to fifty-five per cent." More open chokes will give him more pattern and he will get better results. The 125-pound hunter should use a light gun, not a cannon.

*   *   *   *

HOW TO HUNT GEESE

For the man who hunts geese there is no other comparable thrill. Here is a bird worthy of the supreme effort—noble, wild, romantic and above all, cagey. I have hunted geese all over the North American continent for more years than I like to admit. Yet the challenge of an incoming goose is as potent with me today as it was the day I shot my first goose on the southern Manitoba farm where I was a downy-faced kid.

Whenever you see geese, you can make your own goose hunting. Years ago when I was living at the Vandalia, Ohio, gun club where the

258

Grand American is held each year, I was told by a Dr. Noble of St. Mary's, Ohio, that there was a large flock of geese on the St. Mary's Reservoir. "There are thousands of geese on the big lake, Jimmy—but you can't get near them," he said. I called Harve Monbeck, game warden and goose hunter from Dayton, and we drove up to the reservoir to try to find the feeding place of Doc's geese.

After two days of careful reconnaissance, we found a flock of Canada geese feeding in a farmer's field. We asked the farmer for permission to hunt his field, offering him a share of our geese if we were successful. We dug our pits that evening, after the geese had left, and returned the following morning before daylight. Sure enough, about nine o'clock we saw a thin line of geese heading for our field. My goose call must have helped because they came in, circled twice and set their huge wings over our decoys. We shot our limit that morning and divided our geese with the farmer.

We tried another field on the following day but failed to get a shot. On the third day, we were back at that same field and the geese came in. We had another fine shoot. We hunted this territory for three weeks and had wonderful shooting—just as good as we would have found in Canada or the Dakotas.

As I said before, first locate where your geese are feeding. This is not hard to do with a good pair of binoculars and an automobile. After you have found the feeding place, watch them carefully. They won't feed very long. And after they have left for their lake roosting place, walk over and inspect the grounds. Then ask permission of the farmer to dig your pits, and dig them. Be back again early on the following morning. If you want to be a goose hunter, you must know the lay of the land. Watch every field every day, especially the barley fields, and you will know when new flocks come in.

When geese alight in a field for the first time, they are always cautious of danger. They will swing over the field several times, usually 100 yards in the air, and look over the situation. The old gander (or goose) that leads the flock will be a few yards out in front with neck stretched downward looking for feed and danger. If the leader is satisfied on both scores, he will start honking for all he is worth. The entire flock will now take up the tune and the air will tremble with cackling. It is a sign that the flock is about to come down.

These are my rubber goose decoys which are easy to carry. Don't you agree they look like geese?

Although the old leader has spotted the feed, chances are he won't make a landing right there. He will guide his flock down in some open spot in the field; and then stand motionless with head down for a few minutes to look over the situation. If all seems clear, he will walk to the feed, caution in every step. It is obvious why your pit and blind should be well concealed.

The flock will feed for about an hour or more and then take off for the lake and gravel. Geese must have gravel after they've eaten. If the feed has been satisfactory, the flock will probably return the next morning.

On the next morning, they may come out early. If undisturbed, they probably will make another trip for feed that day. Geese are always hungry. They should return about four or five in the evening, but I have seen them come back around noon. By this time, they will think they own the field. Throwing caution to the wind, they will sail in without even making a circle. If you are a real hunter and have plenty of time to hunt, it is my advice to leave a flock alone for a couple of days. Then you will get your best shoot.

One of our guides told me last year that a flock of geese had landed in a field about two miles from our duck camp on Lake Manitoba. Next morning, Tom Oliver, an old-time trapshot, good hunter and fine shot, and I were on hand with Tom's Bausch and Lomb glasses. The flock came in about nine o'clock. We had no pits so we lay by a fence and studied every movement they made during their feeding. That evening, they returned again and once more we were on hand with our glasses. That evening we dug pits. On the following morning, Wayne Winterburn and Tod Raven, old-timers at the club, joined us. The flock came in at nine. They headed straight for our decoys without so much as making a circle. We left that field alone for several days and another flock made its appearance. It is best not to shoot a field two days in a row, even if the geese do return to it.

Be sure you fill your pits after you have finished hunting a field. Open pits are dangerous to livestock and tractors. Do not shoot with more than two hunters in a pit, if possible. Sometimes we dig several pits, one per gunner, about fifteen yards apart. Don't make your pits too deep. Usually I dig mine about waist high. It should be narrow as possible—giving you just room enough to stand up and shoot.

After you have dug the pit, carry away all the fresh dirt. Scatter a little hay around the edge of the pit. Usually I place a couple of goose decoys at the edge of mine. Make the pits look as natural as the surroundings. If you dig your pit at night, mark the spot well. Otherwise you will have a hard time finding it in the dark in the early morning. Don't leave your car near the pits. It will warn the geese.

Don't look up or move when the geese come in and circle. If they intend to come into your decoys, they will come in with the wind, circle once or twice and then sweep down over your blocks against the wind. When they make that final sweep, within gun range, it is the time to rise and fire.

Always keep cool and pick out a bird. Knock over the leader, if possible; then the others may become confused and swing back. Never jump up for the dead geese after you have fired your first volley. The geese often circle and come back.

Check your gun, time after time, in a dusty goose pit. See that it is always free of dirt. I have seen many a hunter pull up, only to have his gun jam, or have the safe on.

Geese are large and therefore deceiving as to range when in flight. Don't jump up before they are within good shooting distance. Let them come in. I have done a lot of goose shooting in my time, but I still have this happen to me. Geese climb fast so lead them as you would a duck. Shoot them in the head and neck, if possible.

Hugh Mackechnie, one of my Canadian shooting cronies who would rather shoot one Canada goose rather than a hundred mallards, prefers No. 4 shot for geese. He says, "I like No. 4's, but I know some hunters prefer a heavier load. Many favor BBs and No. 2's but this is a matter of opinion." While most hunters use a standard 12-gauge, some prefer a 3-inch magnum, which has about ten yards greater range and a denser pattern. But here is the real secret in goose shooting—let them come within range. You can do it if you are a good caller, prepare a good hide and place the proper spread of decoys in front of your hide.

Usually you will find the white-fronted goose and cackling goose, a miniature of the Canada, wherever you find the Canada honker. This applies to Canada and the northwest states. Hunt them as you would the Canada.

White geese and blue geese, which outnumber the Canada goose, are hunted in Texas, California (whites), Louisiana and the James Bay in Ontario. Locate their feeding grounds as you would the Canada's. They are hard to locate in the southern coastal waters, but easy to shoot when you get among them. In the South, the "marsh buggy" is used to reach the boggy grounds where they feed and rest. Some are shot from duck blinds along the coast.

262

Baker Robbins and Jack Seville shooting Canadas from a pit blind on the eastern shore of Maryland.

There are several kinds of goose decoys. Your choice depends largely upon what kind of geese you are shooting and where you are hunting. Down in Louisiana where Harry Englehart and I hunted with Clarence Faulk, world's champion goose caller, we used white paper decoys. We simply scattered a few pieces of paper, about the size of a goose, on the ground.

The most popular decoys for goose shooting are stuffed decoys, silhouettes, and rubber decoys. The rubber decoys are easy to carry and like the stuffed decoys, make a fine stand. Silhouette decoys, made of either wood, paper or tin, are desirable too. In scattering your silhouettes, be sure you do not have them all facing in the same direction or the geese may not see them as they approach your field. They can see the rubber or stuffed decoys at any angle.

I do not follow any certain formation when I place out my goose decoys. However, I do place them downwind so that when the geese come in against the wind, they won't have to come in over the decoys. I simply scatter my decoys so they look like feeding geese. The more your decoys resemble a goose, both in size and color, the better chance you have of bringing geese within gun range.

Never place your decoys near a fence. Usually geese will light in the middle of the field, too far from a fence for you to shoot them. If you have an extra hunter in your party, place him along the fence between your pits and the lake or at a spot where the geese, retreating from the mid-field fire, will fly over him against the wind. Don't have your decoys standing erect like a platoon of soldiers. Geese don't feed that way. Some of your decoys should have their heads down as if they were feeding. After you have killed geese, prop them up on sharpened sticks among your decoys. Don't leave dead geese lying among the decoys.

Credits for Colored Reproductions

Frontispiece—Black Ducks by ROGER PREUSS *through the courtesy of Louis F. Dow Co.*

Chapter Two—Canvasback by LES KOUBA

Chapter Five—Snow Geese by ROGER PREUSS *through the courtesy of Sports Afield*

Chapter Six—Moose by LES KOUBA

Chapter Nine—Ring-necked Pheasants by ROGER PREUSS *through the courtesy of Shedd-Brown, Inc.*

Chapter Twelve—Quail by LES KOUBA *through the courtesy of Royal Stationery Co.*

Chapter Thirteen—Jets by LES KOUBA

Chapter Fourteen—Widgens by ROGER PREUSS *through the courtesy of Louis F. Dow Co.*

Back Cover—Canada Geese by ROGER PREUSS *through the courtesy of Louis F. Dow Co.*

Photo Credits

Bruce Reinecker	Don Berg
Dick McConnaughy	Jim Peterson
Al Ridinger	Jack Connor
W. P. Mayfield	Sam Nickerson
Walter J. Welwerding	Anthony Lane Studio

Minneapolis Star & Tribune